The Lost Films of
JOHN WAYNE

Also by Carolyn McGivern:

John Wayne: A Giant Shadow
Ronald Reagan: The Hollywood Years

The Lost Films of
JOHN WAYNE

Carolyn McGivern

CUMBERLAND HOUSE
NASHVILLE, TENNESSEE

THE LOST FILMS OF JOHN WAYNE
PUBLISHED BY CUMBERLAND HOUSE PUBLISHING, INC.
431 Harding Industrial Drive
Nashville, TN 37211

Cover design: Bruce Gore Studio
Text design: Lisa Taylor

Library of Congress Cataloging-in-Publication Data

McGivern, Carolyn.
  The lost films of John Wayne / Carolyn McGivern.
      p. cm.
  Includes bibliographical references.
  ISBN-13: 978-1-58182-567-1 (pbk.)
  ISBN-10: 1-58182-567-6 (pbk.)
  1. Wayne, John, 1907–1979—Criticism and interpretation. I. Title.
  PN2287.W36M34 2006
  791.43'28092—dc22
  [B]   2006018261

Printed in Canada
1 2 3 4 5 6 7 — 11 10 09 08 07 06

CONTENTS

• • •

On April 4, 2003, Michael Wayne, "The guardian of his father's legacy," died of heart failure and complications of lupus at age sixty-eight. The eldest of Wayne's seven children, he headed the family production company, becoming president of Batjac Productions in 1961.

At the time John Wayne happily said, "That kid runs a tight ship. He's all business and no nonsense." Maureen O'Hara also recalled him as a tough producer: "I asked Duke once, maybe we should do this or maybe we should do that. He said, 'Maureen, you've got to talk to the boss'—Mike. Duke was very proud of him."

Michael Wayne established Wayne Enterprises to control his father's image and protect his name, including the licensing of various products. He was exceptionally careful about releasing films to TV and video, for years holding back certain films like *McLintock!* and *Hondo*, saying, "I believe less is more. I believe they should have a periodic release rather than being put into syndication. I model myself after Disney. If the public wants to see a picture it hasn't seen for some time, there's more impact with a periodic release."

ACKNOWLEDGMENTS

Many thanks to everyone who has made this book possible: my friend, the late Fred Landesman; Pete Sammon; Katie, Heather, and Chris, Mum and Dad; friends and family too numerous to mention.

●　　●　　●

All stills courtesy of the Academy of Motion Picture Arts and Sciences, the British Film Institute, Fred Landesman, or the author's private collection.

The Lost Films of
JOHN WAYNE

INTRODUCTION

Lost and Found

Hollywood icon John Wayne created a personal treasure trove of films during a fifty-year career that spanned from 1926 to 1976. Today, scarcely an hour goes by without one of his films appearing somewhere in the world on TV listings, on video, or in DVD format. Thankfully for the fans, only a handful remained unobtainable through an era of remastered miracles, and out of all the movies he made after 1939's *Stagecoach*, only two were retained as long as *Island in the Sky* and *The High and the Mighty*. Both movies were kept out of circulation for almost a quarter-century due to a quagmire of legal and technical issues. Finally, *The High and the Mighty* made its comeback when it was rebroadcast on American television in July 2005, and then both it and *Island in the Sky* were released as special edition DVDs that August.

Island in the Sky and *The High and the Mighty* are an unusual "pair" of film oddities, two aerial films made and screened in the mid-1950s when the John Wayne cowboy and war hero box office phenomenon was reaching its zenith. His starring performance in both is legendary, if seldom seen until now. *The High and the Mighty* is also the first in a long line of all-star cast disaster films which focused attention on the personal dramas of the passengers and which set the scene for *Airport* and its sequels more than twenty years later.

Both films are also two of the earliest John Wayne co-productions in which he himself starred. This production practice did not become widespread until the 1980s and 1990s, when stars such as Robert Redford and Clint Eastwood took control of their own productions. Wayne was doing all this some thirty years ahead of the pack.

Both pictures were produced by Wayne-Fellows, Wayne's production company, and directed by William A. Wellman, whose diverse body of work was largely ignored until comparatively recently. Andrew V. McLaglen was assistant director on the pictures, both based on novels by Ernest Kellogg Gann.

Gann, himself a pilot of distinction, oversaw both screenplays, giving them a deep sense of tangible authenticity and continuity. William H. Clothier was aerial cameraman on both films, and he achieved some breath-taking scenes. He later worked on many John Wayne films, including *The Alamo,* and was sometimes referred to as "Wayne's Cameraman."

Hollywood had enjoyed a long-lasting love affair with military pilots, stretching back to the very first Academy Award Best Picture winner in 1927, coincidentally another William A. Wellman movie, *Wings.* Less heralded than those pilots perhaps, but certainly no less important, were the fliers depicted in *Island in the Sky* and *The High and the Mighty.* Here were two massive pictures with casts, crews, directors, and producers of impeccable pedigree, and yet somehow they fell by the wayside and lay unseen for decades. Fortunately they had made a strong enough impression in the 1950s to ensure they were never forgotten, at least by Wayne fans, and it proved to be those loyal fans who eventually perpetuated the legacy.

Warner Brothers had distributed *Island in the Sky* in 1953 and *The High and the Mighty* in 1954, but the rights to the movies reverted to and were held by Batjac Productions, a direct familial descendent of Wayne's independent film production company. Over the years there has notably been some friction between the original distributor of the pictures and the owner of the prints so that although through the sixties and seventies *The High and the Mighty* was sometimes seen on network television, that film's last appearance on American television was in 1982 on the cable channel TBS. *Island in the Sky*, at first glance a lesser film simply because it was shot in black and white, was hardly ever seen after its first theatrical release.

Although strictly speaking the films remained unobtainable for well over twenty years, the Internet has made it possible for the true detectives among us to trace some dreadful pirate prints of both films. The actual films however were hastily withdrawn in the 1980s after the first pirated copies began appearing, and they remained tightly guarded gems until Michael Wayne's widow finally released both to the American DVD market in 2005.

Fans had longed to see them again, and as the power and influence of the Internet grew, so did the voice of those eager to see the rarities. Chat rooms were soon buzzing with questions about where the two movies lay and when they might be seen again. A strong cult following developed, and petitions were organized to get both re-released. When people from around the world left messages on these sites and organized their petitions, they could be pretty sure that Michael Wayne was hearing them. Those short on charity moaned that Batjac Productions was simply fermenting the desire to see the films as best it could by withholding them ready for some future grand release, rather as had happened with the classic *Hondo* some years earlier.

Following the sudden death of Michael Wayne, Paramount Home Entertainment and Paramount's television distribution arm entered into an agreement with Batjac Productions for the worldwide DVD and television distribution of the films under special license. The deal to release the newly restored and remastered lost films, neither of which had previously been released on VHS or DVD, was struck be-tween Thomas Lesinski, president of Paramount Pictures; World-wide Home Entertainment; Joel Berman, president of Paramount Worldwide Television Distribution; and Gretchen Wayne, president of Batjac. Gretchen Wayne's restoration of *The High and the Mighty* sees the film returned to all its former colorful glory in a 35mm widescreen double disc presented in stereo surround sound, while *Island in the Sky* offers a solid full-frame transfer from a restored print that is virtually flawless, with smooth gradients and barely a hint of

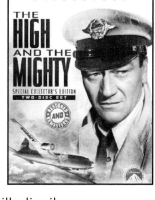

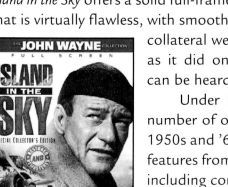

collateral wear, looking just about as crisp as it did on premiere night. Clear audio can be heard on a Dolby 2.0 track.

Under the agreement, Paramount will distribute a number of other rarely seen John Wayne vehicles from the 1950s and '60s, and each DVD will include nostalgic bonus features from Batjac's extensive library of film memorabilia, including commentaries with filmmakers and cast and fea-turettes on the making of the films, their subjects, and their eras, incorporating new interviews, archival materials, and also *The Batjac Story*.

Lesinski, clearly delighted to have orchestrated the release of the lost films, said, "Paramount has enjoyed a wonderful relationship with John Wayne and his family for more than half a century. With the addition of these timeless treasures to our existing John Wayne library, Paramount has truly become the home of John Wayne's films."

Late in his life, John Wayne commented that he hoped people remembered per-haps six of his best pictures and forgot the rest, and for whatever reason these two gems were lost to us all for so long, he can finally rest easy. The last of his classic body of work can be seen again. They now must merit some of the deeper reflection his other films have received over the years, partly because John Wayne is their very special star, partly because they were lost for so long, and very much because they were both of immense value in their own right, deserving recognition as a couple of his best efforts on his own terms.

CHAPTER 1
Independent Production

John Wayne and Robert M. Fellows discuss getting their production partnership started. Wayne-Fellows was a farsighted venture that became a trend among Hollywood stars.

● ● ●

In 1952, at a time he dominated the Hollywood film industry, John Wayne established one of the first independent film production companies. It was an unusual and farsighted venture that soon turned into a trend among the stars of the day. A major box office attraction for Republic Pictures, his contract already gave the Duke a minor say regarding which producers, directors, and scriptwriters he worked with, and up to a point he could pick and choose which roles he wanted.

As Wayne's career as Hollywood's leading man fast approached its zenith, a number of diverse factors spurred his desire for greater independence and diversification, mainly from Republic, but also in other areas of his life. He had suddenly arrived at a complex crossroads, a point where difficult decisions had to be taken, directions changed, opportunities grasped—or it would be too late.

He lived a turbulent, messy, and precarious private and financial life. He and his second wife, Chata, had filed simultaneous divorce suits. He lived in a small rented house on Longbridge Avenue in Sherman Oaks, California, and rented out his Encino estate. He said he had half a million dollars but had no idea how much the divorce was going to cost him. Complicating matters, he had already met and fallen in love with Pilar Palette while searching for remote film locations in Peru. He brought her to Los Angeles and set her up in an apartment close to his own while he maneuvered the sticky proceedings with his wife.

Despite the shambles, Duke continued to seek distraction in the best way he knew, busying himself making pictures and planning the direction his life would increasingly take. Robert Fellows, a producer at RKO, had often worked with John Wayne in the past. Both he and Duke had been around the lots in various capacities since 1926. Between them, they knew the business inside out. When Duke had moved into acting in 1929, Fellows had shifted into production at Warners. Duke said, "What Bob doesn't know about the business isn't worth knowing. He's been a stage manager, actor, assistant cutter, prop man, writer, and director." More importantly he had been a close friend of Wayne's since they first met in 1940 on the set of *Seven Sinners*.

For years Wayne had toyed with the possibility of becoming an independent film producer. He wanted more input in his movies, more financial and artistic license. He was committed to Republic Studios, an outfit he considered scarcely even mediocre, a studio without the financial backing to make the sort of films he dreamed about. Wayne said that though he and Republic boss Herbert Yates had grown up in the industry together, Yates had learned nothing, commenting, "The man has the soul of an accountant."

As soon as he returned to the studio in August 1951, after completing work on *The Quiet Man* with John Ford and Maureen O'Hara, he wanted to get busy working on his own pet project, *The Alamo*. He and Bob Fellows had drawn up a budget to make his film for three million dollars. Yates, who had originally agreed to let them shoot the movie within the Republic set up, hesitated once he saw the budget. He wanted to cut costs and, Duke felt, cheapen his product. He recognized Republic could not produce the film he envisaged and had set his heart on. This led to a final catastrophic showdown with Yates. *The Quiet Man* was the last film Wayne made for Republic.

Wayne said, "Yates will have to make me a darned good offer to get me to do another movie with him. I'm fed up to the teeth with him. I wanted to do *The Alamo* through my own company and release through Republic. Yates told me I would have to give up my company and make the picture for Republic. He told me, 'You owe it to Republic. We made you.'

"How do you like that? I don't owe them one thing. I've made plenty of money for Republic. No I'm not going to give up my own production company. I'm looking for security for my kids."

Duke's dream had outgrown Republic and he needed to develop his own, bigger production facility to keep pace. He had kept his ideas on the backburner, biding his time, but by 1951, time ran out. He was getting older. He believed his time for retirement from in front of the camera loomed. Already into his forties, he was sure he could not continue playing leading men for much longer. He was scared of being forced to drop out of movies and decided to develop a thorough knowledge of film administration. He believed this would facilitate a smooth transition from star to backroom boy, thereby continuing a career in the industry he loved more than any woman. There was no turning back as he stormed out of Republic for the last time.

He had already been producing his own films at Republic and a small unit at Warners. He had teamed up with Robert Fellows in 1950 to produce *The Bullfighter and the Lady*, a film based on the early career of director Budd Boetticher. Wayne had forced Herbert Yates to assign the production a limited budget. The movie was directed by Boetticher himself and starred Robert Stack.

Wayne and Boetticher worked hard and put together an impressive film. Stack said, "There wasn't one phony thing in that film." Both artistically and financially the project was a success, and Duke's plans for his future accelerated accordingly.

Naturally he had learned many lessons from his mentor, John Ford, particularly that making successful movies required teamwork of the highest order. With dogged determination he and Fellows set about assembling a team of artists, technicians, and experts second to none. They were mostly friends or people he really wanted to work with, including script writer James Edward Grant and leading cameraman William H. Clothier. Wayne Fellows began work on a second production, *Plunder of the Sun*, starring Glenn Ford, who was contracted to Wayne-Fellows.

Once he had formerly cut all ties with Republic, it made sense to put his busi-

Deeply troubled, John Wayne with his back to the wall.

ness dealings with Fellows onto a formal footing. Fellows resigned his position at RKO Studios to join the Duke, and they formed independent company Wayne-Fellows. Duke said, "It marked the start of a new era. Sink or swim, it had to be better than working with men like Yates." He continued, "It gave me a little more freedom to do what I wanted. It also gave me a bigger slice of the pie." He went on, "I want to make personal stories. What I look for is a story which a kid of ten and a guy of fifty can identify with. I like folklore. Everyone understands it."

There had always been some independent production in Hollywood, but now, with Wayne's increased activity, the practice gathered importance within the industry. The major studios were all cutting costs, producing fewer pictures and hiring less staff, and there was a decline in contract directors, writers, and crew. At the same time the popularity of the big stars increased, and they became more powerful. The decade after the war saw an unprecedented rise in star-controlled companies. In 1945 there were forty independent producers; by 1957 there were 165.

There were certain perils attached to independent production; without his own distribution arm Duke remained dependent on studios like Warner Brothers, but certainly for Wayne, the artistic and economic benefits of his new venture made everything worthwhile. Most importantly as things stood in his recently divorced state, he discovered his financial rewards rocketing. Duke had never been wealthy. His day-to-day existence was far from extravagant and nothing like his fans would have expected of Hollywood's leading box-office star. The plan in setting up his own company was that he would make creative decisions and Bob Fellows would look after the financial details.

Wayne-Fellows's first business move was conservative, reflecting the trends of the day. Most independents found the risks a little scary and looked to sign multi-picture contracts with a single studio. This made it easier for the company to obtain studio financing as well as distribution. Shortly after going into business, Robert Fellows tied Wayne-Fellows to a similar contract at Warner Bros.

Wayne already had his own agreement in place there. In May 1949 he had signed a lucrative contract to make seven pictures over seven years. He would be paid a salary plus 10 percent of the gross on each film. Part of the agreement was that Wayne's own production unit would be allowed to make films at the studio, which Warners would distribute. Meanwhile, Duke remained free to make pictures elsewhere, and he hoped he would ultimately be given a chance to try his hand at directing.

The new deal that Fellows had signed troubled him deeply. Fellows had agreed to an exclusive seven-picture contract that would prevent Wayne-Fellows from making movies for other studios. Duke thought this negated his becoming an independent, and eventually, after much heated argument, he agreed to sign a five-picture, non-exclusive contract. Warners agreed to finance and distribute Wayne-Fellows productions and to pay Duke $150,000 per film and 10 percent of gross receipts.

Sometime during the early fifties, Duke began his emergence as an increasingly political animal. America's domestic and foreign policies troubled him deeply; he felt under threat, his entire existence in danger from Communism. Through Wayne-Fellows he would be able to make any political statement he wanted to in his films.

While he planned to use his new position as an independent producer for his own political ends, from October to December 1952 he was tied up starring as a pool-shooting, divorced football coach in *Trouble Along the Way* at Warner Bros. He was still mid-divorce and throughout filming he couldn't get his "psychiatric opponent" Chata out of his mind. He fretted about the damage she was doing to his reputation and became short-tempered and given to sudden noisy outbursts. He was difficult to deal with.

Melville Shavelson, producer of *Trouble Along the Way*, had no doubt at all that Chata's activities had the desired effects on her husband. She had put detectives on his tail, and he was "going out of his mind." Shavelson commented, "One day he shook the detective and didn't show up on the set for a week. . . . This affected his work on the picture." The Duke bitterly resented the harm Chata did to his private and public life. "It was an embarrassing ordeal to live through. I think I tried to live in a dignified, respectable way. My life was almost ruined," he said.

The story that continued to interest Duke more than any other was *The Alamo*. He was willing to take on any commitment that would help finance that project. Throughout the fifties, running all through his problems, he was hard at work on *The Alamo*. As much as anything else, Wayne-Fellows became about making enough money to make dreams come true.

The next project Wayne-Fellows moved on to was *Island in the Sky*. Duke's company bought the rights to the best-selling novel by Ernest K. Gann, certain the resulting movie would put money in the bank. Duke then looked around for cast and crew.

Robert Fellows, Duke's friend and coproducer at Wayne-Fellows. Duke called him "the most important member of the team." They talked business and dreamt of taking control.

CHAPTER 2
Island in the Sky

● ● ●

The Wayne-Fellows production *Island in the Sky* concerns the graphic action in 1944 surrounding the crash landing of a four-engine C-47 transport plane in the frozen wastes of Labrador during World War Two. The story concentrates on the efforts of the crew to survive five harrowing days and nights while thrilling rescue attempts are made by search planes.

The factory-named "Corsair," airborne somewhere between Greenland and North America, has carried its civilian pilot, Captain Dooley (John Wayne), and crew to the forsaken portion of a heavy winter sky. The plane is provided by the Army Transport Command, while captain and crew are members of a commercial airline, a satisfactory arrangement for all concerned, particularly the experienced Dooley, who at forty-three would otherwise be tied to an army desk, despite his 15,000 flying hours.

Once on the mission, Dooley is unable to obtain cross bearings and finds himself having trouble flying out a bitter snowstorm. He tells young radioman D'Annunzia to send a message, "Tell them we're in a jam. We're taking a course of thirty-three degrees until our gas runs out."

Hardly an hour had passed before Dooley knew again, as he had so many times before, that feeling close akin to hunger—an emptiness in his digestive parts that became almost nausea. Dooley knew the feeling, knew it every time there was a reason to fear. It came faithfully to all men who flew to live. The face became hot. The temples pounded, not painfully but with noticeable acceleration. The hands became wet. There was a recurrent surge to the feeling. It would mount within the body to an almost unbearable degree, then fade, only to return again with increasing strength. It came when something was wrong—seen or unseen.

You don't worry about rough air; it's just uncomfortable, or even static. You do worry about the winds. They're invisible and can be so powerful. But most of all you worry about ice. It can kill. Have you ever been afraid? It comes like now, when you're going down. Doubt creeps through your mind . . . and you pray. Dooley sensed the feeling in his stomach and hated it.

The buildup of ice and the power of the wind is forcing them down, but fully aware he is carrying his men into uncharted territory, a wilderness, Dooley thinks it will at least be flat up there, easier to crash-land the plane.

WARNER BROS. PICTURES PRESENTS

JOHN WAYNE

in
William A. Wellman's

ISLAND IN THE SKY

General release date: September 3, 1953
Running time: 109 minutes
Length: 9,845 feet
A Wayne-Fellows production for Warner Bros.

CAST

CREDITS

John Wayne, Lloyd Nolan, Walter Abel, James Arness, Andy Devine, Allyn Joslyn, James Lydon, Harry Carey Jr., Hal Baylor, Sean McClory, Wally Cassell, Gordon Jones, Frank Fenton, Robert Keys, Sumner Getchell, Regis Toomey, Paul Fix, Jim Dugan, George Chandler, Bob Steele, Darryl Hickman, Touch (Mike) Connors, Carl Switzer, Cass Gidley, Guy Anderson, Tony DeMario, Louis Jean Heydt, Ann Doran, Dawn Bender, Phyllis Winger, Fess Parker

Directed by William A. Wellman
Screenplay by Ernest Kellogg Gann, from his novel *Island in the Sky*
Photographed by Archie J. Stout, ASC
Aerial Cameraman: William Clothier
Edited by Ralph Dawson, ACE
Art direction by James Basevi
Assistant Director: Andrew V. McLaglen
Production Manager: Nate H. Edwards
Music by Emil Newman
Set Decorator: Ralph Hurst
Script Supervisor: Sam Freedle
Property: Joseph LaBella
Special effects: Alex Weldon
Makeup: Web Overlander
Dialogue recording: Earl Crain
WarnerPhonic Sound: William Mueller
Stills: Don Christy
Technical Advisor: Ernest K. Gann

HE FOUGHT EVERY FURY OF MAN AND MOUNTAIN TO GET WHERE HIS WOMAN WAS!

During any one of the next few hundred seconds, he, Dooley, would cease to live. The Corsair would meet with the planet earth and earth would resist. One thousand feet. His legs were taut as if to catch the impact by themselves.

Rubbing the gray stubble on his chin, Dooley stares into the evening. "I don't like," he mumbles in John Wayne's leathery voice, "the look of that there god-damned cloud bank." Dooley always refers to things as "that there." He is tired. His eyes burn. His legs ache. His tongue is dry. He places an oxygen mask over his face for a moment, breathes deeply, and stares again at the cloud bank ahead. He struggles on until the fuel runs out, ice building up all the time and forcing the plane downward. One thousand feet. Could the ceiling reach the very ground? Dooley eases the Corsair down toward a frozen lake.

"'It better be quick!' Dooley braced himself for death. He'd always wanted it to come this way, or so he'd said."

The crew shout their relief, "We made it! We made it Skipper! Yeah, we're down. Yeah, in one piece!" Dooley breathes a heartfelt "thank you, God Almighty."

The radio station at Presque Isle has received the desperate message sent earlier but has been unable to get position reports; the Corsair can't be traced. The men at headquarters understand they will have 10,000 square miles to search. Colonel Fuller (Walter Abel) comments, "He's at least 200 miles in uncharted country. Even the Eskimos won't have it." He is worried about losing more planes but begins to gather together a search party of Dooley's flying comrades. Five pilots assemble: Moon (Andy Devine), McMullen (James Arness), Stutz (Lloyd Nolan), J. H. Handy (Allyn Joslyn), and Hunt (Harry Carey Jr.). The story turns to each of them as they are given the news "Dooley is down." Each man knows the men will be freezing and starving to death and that something has to be done to save them fast. "We're gonna stick our own necks out a little more than usual," says Stutz. Each one, weary from just-finished flights or back at home enjoying rare family time, is prepared to drop everything to join the search for one of their number.

Meanwhile, with the Corsair squatting "like a huge brown elephant in the middle of the long narrow lake," Dooley worries:

Well, you're down. Yeah. Right in the middle of a big freezing nowhere. Five guys and no food, so you've gotta find food. That's number one. You've got to keep your strength. It's your only chance against this cold. And then to find out where nowhere is, that's number two. Your crew. They're depending on you. They'll listen to you today, and tomorrow maybe, because their bellies are full. But when freeze and hunger hit them, they'll

Nobody had ever seen Dooley scared before. He had nerve to burn— and he'd burned his way to every corner of the globe where no man had ever been before—the white hell of the wasteland. And now against avalanche, hurricane winds and all the fury of man and mountain—he was beating his way back—and he was pulling the guttiest miracle a guy on his own ever dared!

A man didn't need a photo to remember Maggie!

WARNER BROS. PRESENT

JOHN WAYNE in Island in the Sky

From the blood-racing adventure best-seller by Ernest K. Gann, author of 'The High and The Mighty'

LLOYD NOLAN · WALTER ABEL · JAMES ARNESS · ANDY DEVINE · SCREEN PLAY BY ERNEST K. GANN · DIRECTED BY WILLIAM A. WELLMAN · A WAYNE-FELLOWS PRODUCTION · DISTRIBUTED BY WARNER BROS.

ALL ITS THRILLS THRILLINGLY HEIGHTENED BY WARNERPHONIC SOUND

17

start getting ideas. Ideas about living, about home. They'll want to set out on their own, find their way out of nowhere because they're human. But you can't be human. You've gotta be tough. You've got to hold 'em together. On their own they'll die. You've gotta keep them here even if they hate your guts. Help will come.

About seventy gallons of fuel is left in the tanks. If they can start the engine, the generators will give life to the radio. But they only have three days' food rations. Dooley is afraid to sleep in the exposed plane, knowing sleeping men can easily freeze to death.

The interior of the Corsair was a black and comfortless place. The outside wind shook the whole ship spasmodically and then eased, to content itself with rustling the Corsair's thin metallic skin. Dooley lay in his sleeping bag and stared at the

Dooley lies in his sleeping bag, weak and terribly alone.

muted light from the porthole just behind the gas transfer
valves. It was the only luminous patch in the pattern of darkness
about him. He was completely exhausted, yet he could not
sleep. He envied the others, Frank and D'Annunzia, Murray and
Stankowski, locked in each other's arms, each managing with his
companion's warmth to escape his own misery.

. . . There were three sleeping bags and five men. Each bag
barely accommodated two men; hence Dooley as Captain was
forced to provide his own warmth. He wished that it had not
been so. He almost wished that he was dead, that he had been
suddenly smashed to bits on the landing. He had never imagined
that a human could be so cold. He could feel the others at his
side yet no warmth seemed to escape from them to him. He
shook uncontrollably from his feet to his head. He would make
a determined effort to lie motionless, and then when the shaking
started again he would curse softly and turn over on his side. He
felt weak and terribly alone. He wanted to talk to someone.

The men talk about being scared. Dooley tells them sharply there is nothing to
be scared of. The rescue planes will come. "Somewhere over those mountains,
they're coming. I know they're looking for us. They won't let us down. They must be
near us. They gotta be."

But can they last that long? Dooley has to clamp down on his own overwhelm-
ing fear. The lives of his crew hang on his resolve. They are all depending on him,
and he must hold them together. He is scared of saying the wrong thing. Their condition is rapidly deteriorating, and Dooley feels angry because he has to be tougher
than he feels, rougher with the men. "Have you ever hit your own kid?" he asks. He
must make sure Murray (James Lydon), Stankowski (Hal Baylor), D'Annunzia (Wally
Cassell) and Lovatt (Sean McClory) survive.

They have a mechanical radio that has to be hand-cranked; Dooley refers to it
as the "coffee grinder." He knows the physical action of cranking it may at least keep
the men warm. It is exhausting work, but he sets up a rotation so they can transmit
their bearings as often as possible. This gives them all hope and the best chance of
survival for the next six or seven days.

Achingly hungry, Frank Lovatt disobeys Dooley's warning to stay in camp and
he sets out alone with a gun to hunt for food. He is soon lost.

Frank nestled more deeply into the snow cavity he had
made for himself. He did not care any more now. The final sur-
render was easy. He was fully aware that in a few hours he

Taking turns with the "coffee grinder," the manually operated radio.

would be dead, and yet it didn't seem to make any difference. He was not cold. That had passed. When he first realized he was lost, he had fired five cartridges, hoping that Dooley and the others might hear him . . . after he had fired he waited a long time without moving, but no one came.

He pulled his knees up close to his belly and instinctively pushed his head down toward them.

It was in this position, with his big body clenched as in birth, that Dooley and the others find Frank the next morning . . . not fifty yards from the camp.

(In the film Dooley fires a gun to call Frank in. In Gann's novel it is Frank who fires the gun to give warning to Dooley. Either way, the sound of the gun is lost in the howling wind.)

Dooley and the crew bury Frank in the snow, saying, "Well, we found our lost man. We found him, but Frank's spirit had already reached his island in the sky.

"When doubt creeps through your mind . . ." All men who fly for a living know fear that gnaws like hunger.

They usually say how good a guy was when they do this, but it seems to me that's for strangers. There are no strangers here. Just one thing to be said about Frank. He was a good pilot. That takes in a lot of things."

No John Wayne screen image ever had to battle the elements of fear and despair more than Dooley. Other Wayne heroes may mention being afraid, but Dooley has nowhere to hide; he has nothing left but the hope of survival. Other Wayne heroes may dissolve fear by firing a gun, delivering a good punch, or staring down the opposition. Dooley, exposed as he is to the brutality of nature, is limited in the responses he can make. He has to focus simply on not surrendering. He and his crew are totally dependent on the actions of others to rescue them and his ability to hold them together.

On the ground the search planes are heard in the distance, closing in, finally almost on top of the camp. The stranded men eventually see them overhead and believe they must be saved, but Dooley can't manage to light a big enough fire to signal to them as the wood is frozen through. The radio batteries are almost dead, and he can no longer send bearings.

In a second's space, Dooley was looking straight up at them . . . it couldn't be. Dooley clenched his fists. He could feel his heart pounding . . . pounding even louder than the engines. And then before any of them fully realized what had happened, the ships had passed. . . . The sound of their engines melted quickly in the twilight. Dooley, without realizing what he did, reached out a futile hand toward them, to the sky. He ran a few steps after them, pleading . . . as if he might stay them.

His voice broke. He stopped and watched them disappear into the dusk.

When the planes had passed over them Dooley had felt limp and a little sick. No one said very much. Dooley studied the dirty, haggard faces. . . . It was strange how they, though four men, had been welded into one spirit by their ordeal.

They were men welded into man and in this process they lost their identity. . . because every urge but survival had been reduced to nothing, they had become a mutual will. Yet this strength was as tricky as it was powerful. . . . A leader had only to falter, a member of the unit to say the wrong thing at the wrong time, and the whole thing would explode and be gone. Dooley was aware of this.

Despite everything Dooley is confident the rescuers will be back. At base, the searchers try again to work out where Dooley is. They hear the weather is worsening and things seem bleak. They fear having to give up.

One of the men talks to Dooley about missing his wife and child. Dooley makes no response. In Gann's novel the reader has already been told that Dooley is married with lots of kids, but this isn't mentioned in the film.

Meanwhile, partly to keep spirits up, the men continue cranking the radio, sending out a weak message, "Return to same place." The exhausted crew gather flares together in preparation for the return of the planes.

Eventually the searchers pick up the signal, and the planes resume the search through atmospherically building clouds. The planes again pass immediately overhead. This time they spot Dooley and his men. They drop food and blankets with a message that a snow plane will be sent in for them the following day. Dooley looks at a tin of Spam in disgust and throws it away.

In the film it is at this point that the audience finds out about Dooley's wife and kids. "Hey, Dooley. I didn't know you had a wife and kids."

"Yeah. Six of 'em."

Dooley fires his gun to call Frank Lovatt back to base camp, but his copilot is already lost to the blizzard.

"When one of your kind is down it becomes so important to the age-old battle that he rise again."

KIDS! FLY YOUR OWN PLANE
with JOHN WAYNE!

Airplane cut out along outline and folded on center dotted line. Fold is then clipped in front with paper clip. Bend down wings and the tail surfaces on the dotted lines. Plane is grasped between thumb and forefinger just below clip, and launched by sailing it into the air with a gliding motion.

[THEATRE IMPRINT]

IT FLIES! REAL MODEL AIRPLANE!

Mat Available for Your Own Local Printing. Carries Art and Type As Shown. ORDER MAT "ITS—501X" from National Screen.

CHAPTER 3
Production Notes for
Island in the Sky

● ● ●

Island in the Sky, featuring a number of Wayne's closest friends and top talent—Paul Fix, Harry Carey Jr., Andy Devine, and James Arness—and directed by fine, old-time filmmaker William Wellman was shot on location at Truckee, Donner Lake, northern California, and at Burbank Studios between February 2 and mid-April 1953. It had an original budget of $900,000 but was completed at $962,000. Filming finished in twenty-one days instead of the scheduled thirty, marking it the second consecutive picture Wayne-Fellows brought in under the wire. Previously, *Plunder of the Sun* was wrapped six days under schedule.

WILLIAM WELLMAN, DIRECTOR

Wayne-Fellows had contracted with William Wellman to make six pictures for the company, three with Duke and three with other stars. "I started out like a racehorse with *Island in the Sky* and *The High and the Mighty*," the director said, "then fell on my skinny butt." Wellman was better with action than character development, but at their best his pictures had muscle and were always visually exciting.

Wayne admired him greatly and on *Island in the Sky* accepted the director's tough, noisy approach without too much difficulty. "He's a wonderful old son of a bitch. . . . He had a metal plate in his head from some accident, and he'd go around belting all these big, tough guys, and they'd be afraid to hit him back for fear they'd kill him. Wild Bill Wellman, a wonderful old guy. A fine director. Didn't delve into character as much as some. I'll tell you the difference between directors. Hawks has tremendous patience with people. Ford won't hire you unless he knows he can get it out of you. Wellman figures you're a pro and doesn't bother you much as an actor. If you don't deliver he'll simply cut the part down; it's that easy."

If Wellman fell on his skinny butt and was more bark than bite, he still refused to defer to Wayne's position as producer on the films they made together; when he didn't take kindly to Wayne's interference with his work, he would bawl him out in front of the entire cast and crew. Complex and highly demanding, with a sailor's vocabulary and a pugilist's social skills, he was extremely loyal, treating crew and stars alike. History paints him as roguish and refreshingly unimpressed with Hollywood.

His legendary explosive temper made him an unlikely candidate for success in the studio system, but that is perhaps why he and John Wayne got on so well. His speed, decisiveness, and skill made him a valued commodity to the actor-turned-producer. These were the things Wayne had appreciated right from the start, the things that always kept him on his toes, bright and interested.

Born into a middle-class home in Brookline, Massachusetts, on February 29 1896, William Augustus Wellman looked ferocious almost from birth. Through his distinguished World War I career—at age nineteen he was a flier in the French Army's Lafayette Flying Corps—he had earned the nickname "Wild Bill." Aviation remained critical throughout his life. Wellman's son later said, "Dad was a dashing, hell-for-leather young maverick."

Married five times, his stormy career ran through the 1930s to the late 1950s, making more than seventy-six films in his thirty-five-year career. He earned thirty-two Oscar nominations. His work was noted for its powerful use of sound, and he helped pioneer today's cinematic language. He sank his own life experiences into his work. He worked with most of Hollywood's top stars and was recognized as a fine director of females.

He started his film career working as a mail boy at Goldwyn, rising to director in the twenties. Douglas Fairbanks Jr. had taken a shine to the World War I flying ace when Wellman was shipped home to America after being shot down. He gave him his first acting job in 1919 in *Knickerbocker Buckeroo*. After seeing it, Wellman told Fairbanks he was finished as an actor and wanted to be a director. Fairbanks then helped him get started at Goldwyn Studios. In the years that followed he said, "I've been fired from every major studio in Hollywood except Disney . . . they never hired me!"

He attempted every film genre with every top star: tough gangster movies, like *Public Enemy* (1931) with James Cagney and *Hatchet Man* (1932) with Edward G. Robinson; action pictures like *Call of the Wild* (1935) with Clark Gable; the definitive Hollywood-on-Hollywood picture, *A Star Is Born* (1937); comedy gems such as *Nothing Sacred* and *Roxie Hart* (1942); Westerns like *The Ox Bow Incident* (1943); and World War II classics like *GI Joe* in 1945.

William A. Wellman, director.

Despite the Oscar nominations, Wellman's work has been largely underrated or ignored through the years. In fact, particularly in the aerial suspense dramas he made with Wayne, he left a personal signature behind, but because neither *Island in the Sky* nor *The High and the Mighty* have been readily available to Wayne fans, two of his finest films were unseen for years. They might have been lost and forgotten altogether if Wayne himself hadn't been their star producer.

Wellman's heroes were an assorted bunch of adventurers, always tenaciously possessive of their freedom, always firm and independent, and they often dealt with camaraderie between professionals in the face of danger in films full of action. Many say he was like Ford in his artistic temperament, while others say that he was much more fun than Ford and less limited to being a man's director. He certainly matched Wayne's own creative preferences.

When Wellman first embarked on his profitable association with Wayne and Warner Brothers, he was already rounding out his directing days in Hollywood and creating his parting moments of brilliance. Wayne generously allowed him creative freedom, and Wellman commented, "He leaves you alone, and that's more than any director could ask for."

Today, his work, while possibly less well known than that of other directors of the era and after years of relative neglect, is beginning to make a critical comeback, particularly the last seven films that were shot by cameraman William Clothier. Clothier said of the director, "Nobody told him how to do anything. He was his own man. He got the people he wanted, and by God, he made the picture. I don't think he cared whether he was classed as one of the great directors. He had the pictures to prove it.

"Bill Wellman would come on set in the morning, and he'd have a piece of paper. He had every shot down there that we were gonna make that day. When we finished the list, the day's work was over. He didn't go on the set and say, 'I wanna rewrite this.' When we started a picture we knew every shot that was going to be made. John Ford was the same way. Wellman took nothing from nobody. He couldn't care less what people thought about him—producers, critics, heads of studios."

In 1996 film critic Kenneth Turan wrote in the *LA Times*, "The films of a complete professional like Wellman find themselves farther and farther from the limelight. But for those who worked with him, the man is harder to forget." Even forty years after his last film, people like Clint Eastwood and Robert Redford are awed by the cantankerous individual. Even Nancy Reagan recalls that the man "could be very intimidating."

Despite intimidation and discomfort, Wayne himself was apparently happy to leave things to the director. In one scene in *Island in the Sky*, he had Duke in the middle of a frozen field set up in Stages 4 and 5 at Goldwyn digging for moose grass. As the captain of the downed plane, he is doing his best to keep his crew alive. He is searching for fuel to keep the small fire alight. "Now, Duke," Wellman says, "you're cold, boy . . . real cold. This blizzard will blow across and help, but I want you to give me all the cold you can give me."

"Cinch," Wayne replies frostily.

The set has been refrigerated by Art Director James Basevi. A huge canvas hose is piping cold air constantly, and the temperature is down to ten degrees. Wayne was not kidding when he said it would be easy to look cold.

Digging for moose grass on the freezing ice-bound set, built on Stage 5 at the Goldwyn Studio.

With the camera ready, the lights shining down from the crosswalks, and the wind machine in place, Wellman gives the signal. Liquid snow is tossed in front of the wind machine, and the blizzard is going strong. Wayne fights the solid-packed snow and the moose grass and finally stumbles out of the scene.

"Cut" is called, and in that instant actor is replaced by the producer, "What's next, Bill?"

Without pause Wellman says, "We move down here and grab a shot of you stumbling this way."

While the scene is being prepared, Wayne keeps a sharp eye on the work going on round the set. "Hey," he bellows at the special effects men repairing the footprints he had left behind, "that won't be necessary. We won't see them in this blizzard anyway." Special effects were finished in half the time it would have taken because Wayne knows his way around the back of the camera: "When you have been around pictures as long as I have you pretty much know the right and wrong way to do things."

His crew was reassured by his own economy and high efficiency; most had already worked with him many years and knew that the only way to stay on a Wayne picture was to know their business as well as he knew his. He was a boss who had all the answers. "You can't fool Duke," said Web Overlander, Wayne's longtime makeup man. "We play more than any other company in Hollywood, but when there's work to be done, it's done fast and it's done right."

Between scenes Wayne is all over the place, helping electricians move lamps, assisting cameramen moving gear, and chatting with the assistant director, Andrew McLaglen. "Andy, are we all set with the extras tomorrow?"

"All set," McLaglen replies.

Wayne would wait for no one and told McLaglen that if he had problems with anyone to just replace them.

When Wellman called, "Let's go," Wayne dropped his coffee, stopped the chat, and ran back. "Let 'er rip."

The storm immediately blows up again and Wayne drags himself toward the camera through three feet of snow, fighting the blizzard and clumsy footing. The instant the shot gets the okay, it's Wayne's voice that orders, "We're finished here. Move to the other end of the stage."

At his command, things happened. A team of men, led by a producer, shift from one end of the stage to the other. Lights, camera, cables, everything is moved. Out in front, alone, pushing an arc light is Wayne. Asked how he likes producing and acting, he smiles and says, "Acting is still a lot of fun. Producing is a real headache. I hope nobody catches cold on this damp stage."

DONNER LAKE

Island in the Sky still ranks as one of the coldest Hollywood pictures ever produced; snow and ice play such a major part of the story that Wellman, Wayne, and McLaglen all kept one worried eye on the calendar and the other on the sky, fretting as they waited for snow to arrive. When it failed to appear, Wellman called Wayne and suggested he and McLaglen try Donner Pass to see if it was any better up there. In the Pass they walked through deep snow until they came to a secluded valley that had everything they needed. The valley, which in the summer served as a runway, stretched out nice and flat for over 6,000 feet and was surrounded by pines identical to those in Labrador. Wayne knew this was ideal.

The majority of the movie was shot in six-foot drifts far enough from civilization to insure they had privacy. In 1953 the mountain area, six miles from Truckee in the Sierra Nevada of northern California, was also primitive enough to lend authenticity for all the desolate outdoor scenes. When the location had originally been selected, with the help of the California Forestry Service, Wayne believed they would get plenty of silence in the area. A runway and road were cut out of the snow high up into the backcountry to make sure the scenery and sound (especially as the film was made in WarnerPhonic Sound) were accurate. However, as the star producer soon discovered, sound can behave in odd ways in snow-covered mountain areas, and the noise of the diesel trucks roaring their way along the Reno-Nevada Highway could clearly be picked up ricocheting round the mountain tops by the sensitive microphones. Railway drone could also be heard in the distance. Wayne said, "The only saving grace was that when it was quiet, it was *really* quiet, the quietest silence I *ever* heard."

WILLIAM CLOTHIER (ASC), AERIAL CAMERAMAN

Wayne's cameraman William H. Clothier (ASC) thought so too. Born February 21, 1903, in Illinois, Clothier died January 14, 1996. He grew up in Decatur, Illinois. Following the end of World War I, at age sixteen he hitched a ride to Texas, where his father worked as a baker. From there he traveled west to Hollywood where his sister was married to a cameraman. "I was standing outside of Warner Bros., wondering what I had to do to get inside, and I recognized this guy walking out. He was from Decatur and was working at the studio as a painter." He got Clothier inside and also got him work as a painter at the studio for a while. Eventually he became head painter at Alexander Studios where the six-day Westerns were shot. There he landed work as an assistant cameraman. He was one of seventeen assistants who worked with William Wellman on *Wings* in 1926.

In 1933, during a sound technician's walkout in a labor dispute, Clothier (who was also a pilot) was asked by RKO to help out by flying over the studio to help shoot exteriors. He did it for one day, and when the dispute ended, he was out of a job. He took employment flying a plane to Mexico, where he met up with an editor and started working with him on a film. The director, a Mexican, was going to Spain to do some work. Clothier went with him and remained there working as a director of photography until 1938.

He spent World War II with the U.S. Army Air Corps, flying combat missions out of England. He was discharged as a colonel. After the war he did a number of second unit assignments involving aerial photography, including *Jet Pilot* for Howard Hughes, another movie starring John Wayne.

He retired in 1972 after gaining two Academy Award nominations for John Wayne's *The Alamo* and John Ford's *Cheyenne Autumn*. During a thirteen-year period he won nine Best Western Picture of the Year Awards.

ANDREW V. McLAGLEN, ASSISTANT DIRECTOR

In the formidable credit list of *Island in the Sky*, outstanding director Andrew Victor McLaglen, son of John Ford's famous stock actor, Victor, was assistant director. Born July 28, 1920, in Walthamstow, London, McLaglen tended to concentrate his talent on outdoor films but had also worked as production assistant on *The Quiet Man*.

His background, growing up and developing around the likes of John Wayne, John Ford, and Wellman himself, and reared in show business meant that he was all Hollywood product, with a well established, acute, and solid insight into movie industry problems.

He said, "I met John Wayne with my father when I was nineteen or twenty. I knew Ford's children, so I was up at Ford's home quite a bit. Wayne had already left Josephine and was married to Chata.

"I was a young man then, but let me tell you, he was bigger than life. He knew the movie business totally."

McLaglen was one of the last of the old Hollywood brigade, a link between them and the new film school wave. He had worked with Wayne in 1945 at Republic on *Dakota* and also on *Sands of Iwo Jima*. Although his initial success lay in TV, he later moved into features. He understood and naturally became very involved in promotion angles.

As John Wayne developed his production company, he had a special interest in younger, hand-picked directors like McLaglen. The actor's views may not have always been deferred to by the likes of tough old birds like Wellman, but Wayne felt there would be more respect from younger directors. McLaglen understood Wayne's position: "There's no doubt he knows what he's doing. He's been doing it long enough." When Wayne was asked if he directed Andrew McLaglen's direction on their films together, he admitted he occasionally made suggestions but that he always knew there was only one boss on a picture.

Respect flowed both ways. In fact, McLaglen eventually directed Wayne in more films than anyone except Ford, Robert Bradbury, and Henry Hathaway. McLaglen said, "Duke knew I wanted to be a director, and he helped me break into it. I had directed 116 episodes of *Have Gun—Will Travel*, ninety-six *Gunsmokes*, and fifteen *Rawhides*. Then he decided he wanted me to do *McLintock!* That was my stepping-stone into big features. I considered him a close friend."

ERNEST K. GANN—AUTHOR, SCREENPLAY WRITER, AND TECHNICAL ADVISOR

Ernest K. Gann developed a keenly successful formula for authenticity when he started writing about the things he knew and understood. He had already written hundreds of stories before getting anything accepted by a publisher. He served as a pilot during World War II, flying troops and equipment all over the world. In 1944 he wrote his first best seller, *Island in the Sky*. "I was able to find time to write the book because I don't like to play cards. I'd write whilst the other pilots played poker."

Island in the Sky is a story about professional pilots, Gann explained, "their special, guarded world—their island in the sky." In the foreword of the book he says that before takeoff, a pilot is keen, anxious, but unwilling to allow people to read his true feelings. He is elaborately casual. He is about to enter a new but familiar world.

The process of entrance begins a short time before he leaves the ground and is completed the instant he is in the air. From that moment on, not only his body but his spirit and personality exist in a separate world, known only to himself and his colleagues. As the years go by, he returns to this invisible world rather than to earth for peace and solace. "There also he finds a profound enchantment, although he can seldom describe it." Perhaps this could also be used as a good description of John Wayne's existence and enchantment within the film world; was Hollywood Duke's own island in the sky?

The project of turning Gann's novel into a movie was proudly remembered by William A. Wellman:

> I hadn't met Ernie Gann, but they got hold of the story. I'd signed a contract with Wayne-Fellows, which was Duke Wayne's corporate setup, for six pictures. The first story they had bought was Ernie Gann's *Island in the Sky,* and they sent it to me to read.

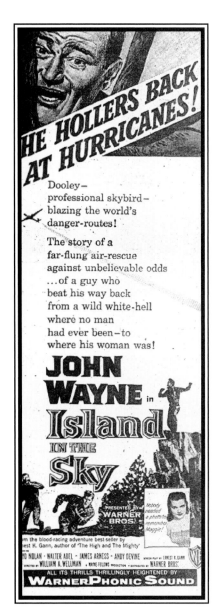

Wonderful. His writing about anything to do with the air is absolutely tops to me. And so we worked on the script together. The only thing I can tell you is that it's a true story and every one of the characters was really true. There was a flier down, and they all left everything; they left their wives, they left their kids. You saw the story; I can't tell it any better than it was done. And they went up in there, and they found him. That's the whole story. They gave everything up to find a pal. And that was fliers.

Wayne and Fellows quickly caught Wellman's enthusiasm. Gann received a check for $5,000 from Warner Bros., and he went to work with Wellman crafting the screenplay. Gann's literary agent, Lester Linsk, had already received payments from both Stanley Kramer and Robert Stillman, who had held an option for a year and then dropped it, then from Twentieth Century Fox, who had also bought the rights before allowing the option to expire. When Warner Bros. issued their check, Linsk quipped, "I hope they don't get around to making this picture. If they do, we'll lose an annuity!"

The completed script about the professional airline pilots who became attached to Army Air Transport Command gave Wayne one of his most heroic screen portrayals. Gann explained, "The men were of the army but not in it. Flying alongside regular army pilots, they continued to wear their usual airline uniforms when conditions permitted, which was seldom. Extremes of cold and heat, the dirt and rigors of far-flung operations, reduced them often to an identifying cap. The story of the Corsair and its occupants is based on a true incident. . . . There may be many more, but no matter what one had been selected and wherever on earth it might have taken place, the men involved would be much the same as Dooley, Stannish, Stutz, and Willie Moon."

Obtaining the film rights to the book and acquiring the services of a top director may have been easy, but getting Gann's script past Joseph Breen, Director of the Production Code Administration, was not all smooth sailing, however. On December 11, 1952, Breen wrote to Jack Warner outlining several problems: the word *damn* had to be removed from all pages; the word *nuts* was on the list of unacceptable words and had to be omitted; the word *jeez* had to be removed; *hell* and *helluva* were also unacceptable. On the other hand, Breen agreed that the overall story generally conformed to the

Ernest K. Gann

provisions of the Production Code. He withheld his final judgment on the project until he saw the finished movie. Gann made his final alterations accordingly and completed the screenplay for the Warner film. The movie was shot and despite earlier difficulties was finally passed acceptable for release by Breen.

Gann not only wrote the story and the screenplay, he also served as technical advisor and did some of the flying in the picture. He had himself piloted transport planes and took over many of the scenes that required precision flying. He flew the large DC-3 as low as twenty feet over the actors' heads. He explained his fascination with pilots. "Flying is hypnotic, and all pilots are willing victims of its spell. Their world is like a magic island in which the factors of life and death assume their proper values." Professional pilots are, of necessity, uncomplicated, simple men. Their thinking must remain straightforward, or they die—violently. Regardless of the world's condition, flying is their life.

THE GIRLS

Gann didn't overload *Island in the Sky* with female parts; the women stay home and pray for the speedy return of the men. Their roles were small but all strong. Ann Doran, a leading Hollywood character actress, played Andy Devine's wife. It is she who has to call Devine away from a swimming trip with his sons to tell him, "Dooley is down." She completed her crying scene in half a day. Dawn Bender, a rising star, played the sleepless wife of downed young navigator James Lydon. Phyllis Winger made her screen debut as Sean McClory's girlfriend. When McClory falls asleep in the snow, he is dreaming of the happier times he has spent with her.

Winger, a nineteen-year-old brunette from Nebraska, had been spotted while auditioning for a small theatre group which entertained returning army veterans in San Francisco. She was selected for the role after an audition with Wellman and producer Robert Fellows. Duke was so impressed with her debut he signed her to a six-picture contract.

ARCHIE STOUT (ASC), HEAD OF PHOTOGRAPHY

Wellman selected Archie Stout as head ground cameraman on the film. He had shot many John Wayne movies, dating back to the earliest Westerns, and he was recognized as the foremost outdoor cameraman in Hollywood. He had been in the game since 1914. Wellman knew he needed an "old innovative pro" to capture the outdoor effect he wanted, so he went to someone "who knew how to be careful." William Clothier also respected Stout's work deeply, and they had often worked together: "Archie influenced a lot of my work. He understood everything about filters."

Duke and costar Phyllis Winger
take a coffee break.

Archie Stout

Light and filters were going to be a major consideration on the picture, and Wellman explained, "The sun reflecting off snow can cause no end of heartache. Stout is an artist with reflectors." Archie himself later wrote, "In my thirty-seven years as Hollywood cameraman, my toughest assignment was *Island in the Sky* for Warner Bros. My champion problem child.

"First of all it had to be shot in subzero weather on location. Second, airplanes were involved, and once that happens there are headaches for cameramen." "Subzero weather" doesn't tell the whole picture, for with it come the companion ills of snow, frost, and ice. In normal cinematography operations there are eighty-seven places in each scene where it is possible to spoil a take. This calls for an excellent crew, a crew who can't do their work in fur-lined mittens. They must use gloveless hands to make the minute camera adjustments. Stout explains:

> The camera is a highly intricate piece of machinery. In extreme cold the metal contracts and refuses to function normally. We had to "winterize" the cameras. All grease and oil are removed because these solidify. In their place we put sperm oil and kerosene to help reduce gear noise and lubricate gears and bearings.
>
> A heating plate was used to try to maintain even temperature in the camera. To do this a generator has to be kept running at all times. Film is also a very sensitive material. In cold it becomes brittle. Somehow it has to be maintained at a similar temperature to the camera, so the magazines are wrapped in padding until they are required. On the other hand, if they get too warm moisture would condense and the cameras would be in real trouble.
>
> Lighting in the snow is another contributor to ulcers. Sun reflection bounces into the lens constantly. Clouds move in and light plummets. Shadows that before looked normal plunge to black, making the snow appear even whiter than in brilliant sun. The only thing we could do was expose for the shadows and the highlights took care of themselves.

Planes have been involved in many films. I have personally worked in over fifty of them, but never like we used them in *Island in the Sky*.

At the climax of the picture, four DC-3 planes, which have been searching the wilds of Labrador, locate the downed ship and buzz the area. They circle again and drop supplies. We had to shoot the scene from three different angles: a long shot from a nearby mountain, a shot from the viewpoint of the men on the ground, and the third from the plane's viewpoint. Of the three, I will long remember the difficulties from the ground up. Have you ever been in the path of four DC-3s flying twenty-five feet off the ground? It's frightening. We used two cameras to do the scene, and it had to be done several times before we got what Wellman was after.

Three hundred eighty-nine camera setups were used to make *Island in the Sky*. Of those, 297 were done in one take. On location, only five setups required more than two takes. Stout photographed scenes to diffuse the blacks and whites. Critics considered it one of the best-photographed films of 1953.

Stout continues, "Our problem was one I had never been up against before. The planes flew so low they caused the cameras to vibrate. Since we were on location, 600 miles from Hollywood and from the equipment we needed to solve the problem, we had to sort something out. We tried securing the camera to a six-foot pine tree. This would provide a certain amount of sway to absorb the shock. The result was excellent.

"In years to come when discussions get around to tough assignments, I will look no further than *Island*, but it was a wonderful picture to have worked on. A cameraman is no better than the crew he works with."

A second photographic unit spent twelve days shooting planes over Oakland airport. Bill Clothier also worked on this. The work is rated some of the best ever filmed. Army Air Corps photographic units have requested permission to use the film as a teaching aid to instruct army aerial photographers in the possibilities of motion picture camera work.

MUSIC AND MAKEUP

Emil Newman, Hugo Friedhoffer, and Herb Spencer composed the music. It was recorded on September 6, 1953, for Decca Records. Orchestra direction was by Emil Newman.

Web Overlander, make-up man for Wayne-Fellows Productions, had worked in the business for thirty years, but in Truckee he found himself making up the airplane. One scene required Wayne to stand by the downed plane. Sun and snow cast a bad reflection on the plane, which every department present tried to tone down. Eventually Overlander offered his services. He did a quick makeup job and the reflection disappeared.

Overlander, however, did have a beard problem. He was faced with tired, dirty, worn-out faces over a period of five days. He had to make sure that the beards on day three were heavier than those on day two and that when they all returned to the studio, they were all accurately matched up with the correct day.

LOCATION

Various other minor problems and complications frustrated the Wayne-Fellows production, but Production Head Nate Edwards eventually managed to get sets sorted out with the help of Art Director James Basevi.

Over the weekend of January 31 through February 1, the great safari began. Chartered planes left Lockheed Air terminal in Burbank and flew the ninety men, cast, and crew to Reno, where they were transported the next forty miles to Donner Lake in two chartered buses and, from there, by five army weasels, designed to float over the snow. The players and crew were based in a couple of resort hotels, Donner Lake Lodge and the Gateway Motel.

No time was wasted, and production started early the next day. The cast and crew went up into the wild mountain valley, and from that point towing sleds carried them two more miles over deep snow to the shooting site, where pilot Bill Wood of Transworld Airlines casually landed a DC-3. Huge tractors had had to run back and forth packing down snow to make a landing strip for him. Wood made a gentle approach and set the plane down, and it stayed there, becoming the center of many of the film's most dramatic moments.

John Wayne, Sean McClory, Jimmy Lydon, Wally Cassell, and Hal Baylor were the only cast members faced with the freezing location trip. Production schedules called for fifteen days, and after the first one the actors agreed this was going to be a tough assignment.

Severe snow storms and gales interrupted filming many times, and hazardous ground conditions added to the strenuous difficulty of filming at 7,000 feet. The threat of further bad weather was a constant worry as Wayne didn't want to extend the shoot. Wellman was quickly forced to abandon the original schedule, saying he'd "shoot while the shooting's good." As a team, actors and crew began a beat-the-weather campaign that had remarkable results. Within just six days, all necessary location filming was complete.

The downed crew spot the search planes for the first time.

Although on location only six days, Wayne still found time to indulge one of his favorite pastimes, and more than once when he had completed shooting, the star gathered string and hook and an axe to move out onto the frozen lake for some quiet ice fishing. There is no report of his success at the hole, but Lloyd Nolan confided that Wayne made a sign which he carried everywhere with him; it read, *Don't ask me what I caught. I'm likely to tell you*.

As was so often the case, Wayne himself became the first casualty of the location. He didn't like to wear sunglasses and stubbornly refused to take medical advice between takes. The sun's reflection off the snow damaged his eyes, and they became very inflamed from the glare. His right eye became very swollen, and for a couple of days he had difficulty seeing. Eventually he received treatment from a local doctor for the problem.

One puffy eye didn't prevent him being voted "Outdoor Man of the Year" by the female members of Donner Ski Lodge, and he was presented with a pair of skis by committee member Ginny Sears, who told him, "We voted you the Outdoor Man of the Year, Mr. Wayne, but we also voted that you wouldn't be at all bad indoors either."

The locals at Donner Lake soon got used to the constant stream of visitors to the set but were amazed the day Hollywood arrived to manufacture its own snowstorm for McClory's death scene with three 200-horsepower wind machines. These kicked up winds of an estimated ninety mph. (After it was all over, McClory couldn't talk for two days due to the force of air on his throat.) One visitor laughed, "Would be great if we could turn our storms on and off like this."

Adding to the fun of the last day of filming, the planes buzzed the whole area. For special effect this was done at between one hundred feet and twenty-five feet, just clearing the branches of the tallest trees. The planes had to circle and drop supplies to the downed crew. This required a number of takes, but when Wellman had finished he exclaimed, "That's the greatest hunk of flying I've ever seen!"

Tim and Mike Wellman, sons of the director, made their screen debuts in the film playing Andy Devine's sons. They were given their chance because the scene called for expert swimmers, and Wellman hated the responsibility this could have created with other youngsters.

INTERIORS

Back at Studio 4 the interiors of four DC-3 planes waited for their call to action. The cockpits were just big enough to squeeze in a pilot and copilot. Great concern mounted when Andy Devine reported for his first day's work as the pilot of one of the ships. Andy weighed in at 285 pounds; no one knew if he would fit into the cockpit, let alone the seat. In the film, the buddy of Wayne's spots the wreck and leads rescuers to the spot. He is the hero.

And in real life Devine was a pilot, but his own plane had a specially built seat to accommodate his size. When Devine, shown in the photo on the next page firmly wedged in his flying seat, first walked on set, he remarked that it was the end of his two-year hibernation from motion pictures. He had been working in TV but felt he had returned home.

In the picture Wayne and Wellman had insisted that everything, down to the last detail, was authentic, including the seat. When Andy approached the tiny DC-3 compartment, he said to Wellman, "Bill, I just don't think I'm going to be able to make this. Isn't there a way to shoot around me?"

Wellman assured Andy he would be fine, even if he had to carve some extra tonnage off him. So Andy tried it out. His backside hung over the arms of the seat. Flesh was tucked and folded so that during filming at least he looked comfortable. It took two prop men to extract him from the damaged chair after filming!

Another production headache Wayne and Wellman faced was how to maintain the viewer's interest in the rescue crews. There was not much action going on in the cockpits. They came up with the idea of shooting from many positions, but this caused all sorts of problems and Wayne said, "There's only so much that can be done with a set as small as this, but we hope the audience will not be conscious of the dogfight waged to get movement into the camera."

CARL WALKER AND JOE LABELLA, WARDROBE AND PROPERTY

Costumes and props were two areas that generally didn't pose much of a production problem. Carl Walker handled wardrobe, and his main difficulty was getting the proper army flight jacket for the right actor, but at least he didn't have to oversee any design work or have new costumes made; most came from army surplus stores.

Island in the Sky was a propman's dream. Planes limit the props that can be used, but Joe LaBella was head of the Wayne-Fellows Productions property department, and he insisted on realism. He spent two full weeks plowing through army surplus stores to get all the gear he needed for planes and crews. The articles he had the most trouble with were the large cargo parachutes used at the end of the film to drop supplies to the stranded men, and eventually he had to have them specially made up by a local manufacturer. At the end of the shoot, Wayne-Fellows was left with ten parachutes they couldn't get rid of. To this day, they are probably still draped somewhere in Hollywood like weary old battle flags.

SEPTEMBER 3, 1953, PREMIERE

Island in the Sky was tradescreened in August 1953 for *Variety*, the *Motion Picture Herald*, the *Hollywood Reporter*, etc., but its world premiere was on September 3, 1953, at the Hollywood Paramount Theatre. Heralded as the "Supersonic World Premiere," this occasion combined the debut of the film with the fiftieth anniversary of powered flight. Aviation celebrities and national and state dignitaries were out in full force on the night, basking in the top TV and syndicate coverage that Wayne arranged and paid for.

John Wayne arrived at the world premiere of Island in the Sky *at the Hollywood Paramount with a young starlet on his arm.*

Film Bulletin—September 1953

Wayne is in his element in the role of "Dooley," the gutty pilot. It's his kind of picture.

Monthly Film Bulletin (British Journal)—November 1953

The pattern of the film is familiar, but in this case handled with skill and intelligence by William Wellman. Very little departure from the theme of the book. A definite avoidance of over-emotional elements. Well-established spirit of camaraderie between pilots and crews. Superbly shot aerial scenes. Acting all round is good and honors are evenly distributed.

That the film was shot in 6-foot snow drifts at Donner Lake and was supervised by the author accounts for the general atmosphere of authenticity.

Hollywood Reporter—August 7, 1953

A gripping, suspense-laden epic of the air.

Island in the Sky is that rare combination of expert writing, acting and directing that holds an audience enthralled from the opening shot to the close 108 minutes later. John Wayne lends marquee strength and contributes a fine performance. *Island* should become one of the year's heaviest grossers.

This third Wayne-Fellows production marks a giant step forward, placing the outfit amongst the top-ranking independents.

Gann's adaptation is a forceful piece of writing and the film is given a masterful directorial job by Wellman.

Today's Cinema (British)—September 25, 1953

Production pulls no punches as a picture of heroism and hardship. Emphatically American, though narrative has general appeal in authenticity of flying detail, chilling impact. A desperate adventure. All-male. Expert technical work. Sound adventure for popular taste.

Warner Bros. production dedicated to the heroism and resource of air pilots. Dooley rations the food, maintains discipline and keeps his men plugging away at the hopeless task of making radio contact with the outside world. John Wayne has a made-to-measure role as tough Dooley. Plays it with economy of expression and emotion.

Time Magazine

John Wayne plays perfectly the clean and leathery hero that has made him a top box-office attraction for years.

Film Daily—August 8, 1953

With a minimum of excess dialogue and narration, it manages to convey the terror, heartbreak, fear and eventually joy of a small group of men trapped in a snowy wasteland.

New York Times—September 10, 1953.

Occasional suspense . . . erratic and unsurprising . . . On the whole *Island in the Sky* remains a standard reply to an extraordinarily simple challenge.

Unexpectedly the Eastern reviews give an unsympathetic response.

Variety—August 12, 1953

An articulate drama of men and planes . . . a picture that will attract box office attention. With John Wayne heading the cast, it has a name of importance . . . a solid piece of drama. . . . Wayne and the cast of male co-stars and featured players are perfectly at home in their characters.

Sign Magazine—1953
by Jerry Cotter

Wayne is superb as a veteran pilot who subordinates his own worries and fears to concern for his men.

Motion Picture Herald—August 1953
by Jay Remer

Starting with a story that's so simple and straightforward as to be almost transparent, Warner Bros. here present a film that plays on the emotions beautifully. With a minimum of excess dialogue and narration, it manages to convey the terror, heartbreak, fear and, eventually, joy of a small group of men trapped in a snowy wasteland. . . . Wayne plays the leader of the lost crew, giving one of his best performances.

Los Angeles Examiner—April 9, 1953
by Kay Proctor

William A. Wellman's superb direction keeps the drama at an ever-mounting pace and is particularly strong in the painting of individual portraits. Chief of these is John Wayne as the skipper of the lost plane. Wayne, looking and acting the part every inch of the way, is plain great and gives one of his finest performances in his distinguished career.

TEASER AD

NEW PEAK OF ADVENTURE IN THE ENTERTAINMENT SKY!

JOHN WAYNE in Island in the Sky FROM WARNER BROS.

ALL ITS THRILLS THRILLINGLY HEIGHTENED BY WARNERPHONIC SOUND

Mat 203—2 cols. x 3½ inches (98 lines)

Island in the Sky wasn't a huge critical success, and the film was often referred to as static and talky. The picture alternates between convincing action and Duke's pithy axioms on matters eternal. Wayne later insisted Warner Bros. had failed to advertise the movie correctly, and signs of a rift between Duke and the studio hierarchy were soon to become apparent.

The film also marked the beginning of the end of Wayne-Fellows and the ultimate launch of Duke's own company, Batjac. Wayne was under plenty of pressure from Fellows, and he spent hours with his lawyer, Frank Belcher. Fellows and Bo Roos, his financial manager, disliked each other. At a party that Duke threw at Romanoff's for the opening of *Island in the Sky*, Roos announced that he thought Fellows was incompetent and not on the level, that he wanted to crush anyone that got in his way, with no exceptions.

Tall order. All the lead stars stood well over six feet and Assistant Director Andrew McLaglen stood 6'7".
Island in the Sky *literally boasts one of the largest casts in Hollywood history.*

CHAPTER 4
Toward Batjac

• • •

As it turned out, Bo Roos eventually did more professional harm to Wayne, almost driving him into bankruptcy through his inefficiency. Still, the seeds of doubt had been planted in the soil of the Wayne-Fellows partnership, and despite *Island in the Sky* earning domestic rentals of $1,661,000 and $781,000 from abroad, cracks in the long-term friendship between John Wayne and Robert Fellows came under increasing pressure after the film's completion.

Bob Fellows was having marital problems, and both he and his wife, Eleanor, seemed intent on involving Duke in their situation. Of course at the time Wayne was up to his neck in his own divorce and difficult affair with Pilar Palette. Fellows had fallen in love with one of his secretaries and in the middle of January 1954 had told Eleanor that he wanted to leave her. She immediately turned to Duke for support. She begged him to talk sense into her husband. Typically, his response was a brusque, "It's not my business."

She pushed him: "You must approve of it then." He didn't but was horrified that he was being forced to interfere. She kept up the intense pressure until he agreed to attend a mediation session with the couple. Duke was always embarrassed by demonstrations of intimate feeling, his own or other people's—definitely not the stuff counselors are made of. He was deeply resentful of being dragged into the argument, and he stormed out of the meeting, suggesting they settle it themselves.

Finally it was the domestic drama rather than professional problems that forced the two business partners to split. Personal pressure affected every aspect of their business relationship, as increasingly the two men wanted different things. They had come up with a relatively successful business formula for producing outdoor action movies at low cost, but Wayne wanted to do much more than that. He was already dreaming about *The Alamo*. It was the very reason he had left Republic in the first place, but Fellows, with other things on his mind, dragged his heels and refused to commit to Wayne's dream.

John Wayne was a very tough, astute businessman, with strong, efficient production values. Personal problems always took a back seat in his world. Andrew McLaglen said of him, "Anyone who doesn't think John Wayne was smart just doesn't know what he is talking about. He had a college education, and I always considered him to be a very cerebral guy in a lot of ways. He was interested in world affairs and politics and vitally interested in his work. He knew the business backward and forward."

Wayne-Fellows, its principals still trying to work things out, went to work on *Big Jim McLain*, a lightweight piece of anti-communist fluff. Duke starred in the picture and surrounded himself with a cast, crew, and technicians he knew and trusted. Warner Bros. had advanced Wayne-Fellows $750,000 for *Big Jim McLain*, but the

John Wayne, son Michael, and Assistant Director Andrew McLaglen take a break on the set of Hondo, *1953.*

production ran into financial trouble, with costs rising to $826,000. Duke had to beg Jack Warner for personal help.

Up to this point, although the star and the owner magnate had had a variety of well-publicized spats, there was also a long-standing mutual bond between the two. Wayne liked and respected the studio boss, and Warner had welcomed Duke into his fold with open arms, aware the actor's movies carried with them certain profit. But a series of problems now began to take their toll until, by 1956, their seven-picture arrangement had turned sour and they were barely on speaking terms. This deepened the chasm opening up between Wayne and Fellows.

Wayne was increasingly convinced that Warner was trying to cheat him and was guilty of skullduggery. On some other level, he was also angry with Fellows for tying their company to a binding contract with Warner in the first place. Independent producers were always destined to lose large revenues from their films because in most cases studios charged a standard 35 percent distribution fee. Studios like Warner Bros. with no financial stake in a picture felt no great incentive to promote it effectively or, in this case, as Wayne himself would have liked. When the studios did help, they felt entitled to retrieve their investment first before the independent received a penny. As an independent, Duke may have had more artistic control, but he remained at the mercy of Jack Warner and complained bitterly, "Nobody came out with a sizeable profit from doing any deal with Warners."

Screenwriter Niven Busch confirmed, "They had the most foolproof accounting system in the world. Wayne went to Warners, and he *never* made failures, but there he was in red ink! It was a kind of put-down for him."

At the same time that Hollywood's biggest studios faced increasing competition from television and dwindling audiences and found themselves forced to cut costs and ease expensive stars out of long-term contracts and movie houses were closing down across the country, Wayne-Fellows suddenly found themselves in a desperate sink-or-swim environment. They would still have been dependent on others but for the immense personal effort John Wayne invested in his company at this point. A failed marriage and the prospect of a messy future, while distressing, didn't distract him in the same way that Fellows allowed himself to be sidetracked.

"Duke's one of the few surefire box-office things left in Hollywood," Howard Hughes declared at the time. Faced with all this, it is little wonder that Wayne felt highly irritated by those less surefire than he was himself. He became increasingly serious about producing his own pictures, about working on projects featuring other stars, and more determined to pull back from those he believed were no longer pulling their weight.

Like the movie roles he played, Wayne had no trouble speaking his mind, writing letters to the likes of Howard Hughes at RKO that almost burnt holes in the page:

> My racket isn't writing letters any more than answering them promptly is yours. . . . I must get some serious beefs off my chest . . . they are very simple. At the other studios and for my own company . . . I seldom get involved on a picture for more than eight to ten weeks over-all. I am paid top terms for that time. At RKO I wind up giving six months of my time . . . and it's hectic, uncomfortable and unpleasant time . . . for a fraction of the compensation paid me by the other studios. You can resolve this by paying me what the others do for the two pictures I owe you.
>
> It is very obvious to me why RKO has always gotten into trouble from the standpoint of time. No forethought has ever really been given by your studio executives to the proper selection

of properties for me at the right time. Frankly . . . none of them have enough ability or experience to decide upon what represents real showmanship. Their efforts have been devoted to coercing me into pictures that are not ready . . . and not even suitable for me.

Are you aware of the fact that I completed my services on *Flying Leathernecks* for RKO in 1951? Under my contract I should have had my next suitable material ready for March 1952. Any stories I suggested were frowned on. I have had to hold months open. After five months I took a job with another studio.

For three years I have had your two commitments hanging over my head. Both should have been finished a year ago.

One after the other I have lost important pictures because of the great length of time you tie me up. . . . I am speaking of outstanding quality pictures . . . the very essence and lifeblood of an actor's existence.

I guess I've run out of words concerning the situation, but certainly not of feeling.

He was fretful and angry about the incompetence he felt surrounded him, feeling that it was holding him back from working on projects that mattered to him personally. His determination to succeed, or at least to do the things he wanted to do, meant he was now willing to split from friends, business partner, longtime associates and colleagues, his ex-wife, and anything else that stood in his way. He became ruthless in his drive to move on.

Although loyalty meant he stalled a while over his imminent split from Bob Fellows, his partner finally provided the solution to Wayne's headache, offering him a convenient and face-saving way out. Fellows could not recover his marriage and, convinced a divorce was fast approaching, he decided to liquidate his assets. Fellows asked Duke to buy him out. Duke agreed, putting up no false argument.

He needed a new name for the company and for several months used "Fifth Corporation." He didn't like it and eventually settled for Batjak, the name of the Dutch shipping company in his film *Wake of the Red Witch*. Inadvertently, it became transcribed as Batjac through a typographical error on the legal documents. When Duke noticed it he commented, "I like it better with a *k* but it's no big deal. Leave it alone."

On May 25, 1954, he rented an office at 1022 Palm Avenue in Hollywood, and Wayne-Fellows became Batjac.

Through much of 1953, Duke had been working on *Hondo*. Still midway through his divorce he had been distracted and touchy, he kept his head down and tried to stay out of the headlines as much as possible. He was working as hard as he ever had, and by the time *Hondo* was released, he was shooting *The High and the Mighty*, at that time still under the Wayne-Fellows banner.

Early in 1953 William Wellman had heard that Ernie Gann was working on another aviation story. When Gann explained the story line, Wellman told the writer, "Stay there. I'll make the quickest sale you've ever had in your life."

Wellman called Wayne, relayed the plot summary and Duke bought the project on the spot, agreeing to give Wellman 30 percent of profit to direct and Gann $55,000 plus 10 percent for the story and screenplay. He told Wellman at the same time that he wanted to shoot the film in CinemaScope, a wide-screen projection process patented by Twentieth Century Fox.

His 3-D experiment on *Hondo* had failed, but Wayne was well aware that the cinema-going public was looking for an experience they couldn't get at home on TV. Why else would they venture out to the cinema? The CinemaScope camera was fitted with an anamorphic lens capable of squeezing a wide picture on to regular 35mm film. Although the technique required the installation of a wide screen in theaters, the visual effects dramatically distinguished CinemaScope from anything available on television.

The next production was immediately under way. Once his own bitter divorce was finalized, Pilar Palette moved into the Encino estate, but she was quickly made aware of Duke's compulsive need to work and that the driving force in his life was making pictures. Although he hadn't been slated to star in the movie himself, when Spencer Tracy pulled out of *The High and the Mighty* at the last minute, Duke stepped straight into the production, scheduled to go before the cameras on November 12, 1953.

"Duke is one of the few surefire box office things left in Hollywood." —Howard Hughes, 1953.

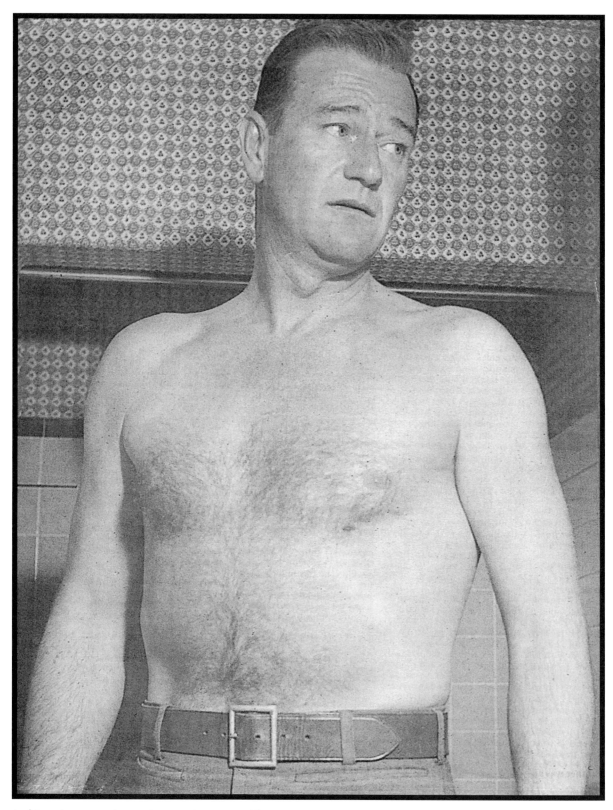

In his prime—and not about to be stopped by anyone.

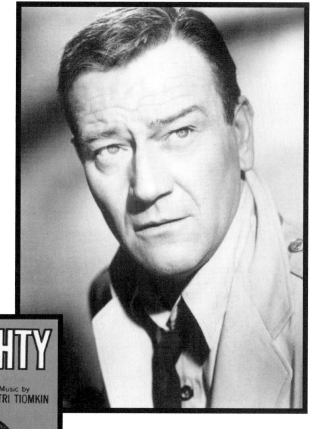

Stepping into The High and the Mighty *as a late replacement for Spencer Tracy.*

Press book (UK) coinciding with the British release of The High and the Mighty. *The booklet included the music score and cost two shillings in predecimal sterling currency.*

CHAPTER 5

The High and the Mighty

The most unusual group of people ever thrown together by fate . . .
"Are you going to declare an emergency?"

● ● ●

The drama-packed story takes place within a twelve-hour, 2,400-mile flight aboard a DC-4. An abnormally bizarre group of five crew and seventeen passengers, all with their own problems, are introduced boarding Trans-Orient-Pacific Airlines Flight 420 from Honolulu to San Francisco as the plane is prepared for takeoff. The weather forecaster points to a chart, shakes his head, and indicates a low pressure belt slipping in from Alaska; there will be serious weather deterioration during the flight. The four powerful engines are revved and a final instrument check is made.

"Sure looks old for a copilot; didn't know we were so hard up," says one of the ground crew watching as Dan Roman (John Wayne) inspects the airplane and whistles a monotonously sad tune.

Roman, the copilot, is a veteran of World Wars I and II and Korea, a barnstormer, and, at age fifty-three, has thirty-five years' experience. He is dealing with the heavy guilt of losing his pilot's license and his entire family when a plane he was piloting crashed. He was the sole survivor of the crash. The forgotten legend, the has-been, turned up to talk to old friend Garfield, Operations Manager of Trans-Orient-Pacific, several years after his luck ran out, to ask for a job, any job. He was assigned that of copilot. He has a pronounced limp and a bleak expression—both cruel reminders of the crash. Mechanic Ben Sneed (George Chandler) tells the young crewman about the tall flier: "Whistling Dan is the only guy I ever knew who had guts enough not to commit suicide." Roman has used up his nine lives and is embarking on his tenth, one where he's left alive to blame himself.

"Hey, fella . . . ain't you Dan Roman?" Ben Sneed (George Chandler) meets up with Dan, "the old pelican," who has already used up his nine lives.

JOHN WAYNE

in

William A. Wellman's

THE HIGH AND THE MIGHTY

General release date: July 3, 1954
Running time: 147 minutes
Length: 13,156 feet
A Wayne-Fellows production for Warner Bros.

CAST

CREDITS

John Wayne, Claire Trevor, Laraine Day, Robert Stack, Jan Sterling, Phil Harris, Robert Newton, David Brian, Paul Kelly, Sidney Blackmer, Julie Bishop, Pedro Gonzales-Gonzales, John Howard, Wally Brown, William Campbell, Ann Doran, John Qualen, Paul Fix, George Chandler, Joy Kim, Michael Wellman, Douglas Fowley, Regis Toomey, Carl Switzer, Robert Keys, William DeWolf Hopper, William Schallert, Julie Mitchum, Karen Sharpe, John Smith, Doe Avedon, Robert Easton, Philip Van Zandt, Walter Reed, Tom Hennesy

Directed by William A. Wellman
Screenplay by Ernest Kellogg Gann, adapted from his novel *The High and the Mighty*
Photographed by Archie J. Stout, ASC
Aerial Cameraman: William Clothier
Camera Plane Pilot: Loren Ribbe
Edited by Ralph Dawson, ACE
Art Direction by Al Ybarra
Special Effects by Robert Mattey
Music composed and conducted by Dimitri Tiomkin
Production Manager: Nate H. Edwards
Assistant Directors: Andrew V. McLaglen, Hugh Brown
Makeup by Web Overlander and Loren Cosand
Hair Stylist: Margaret Donovan
Property: Joseph La Bella
Script Supervisor: Sam Freedle
Technical Advisor: William H. Benge
Sound: John K. Kean
Set Decorator: Ralph Hurst
Color by WarnerColor
Filmed in CinemaScope

Dan Roman moved deliberately through the ritual of pre-flight inspection. He was a lean rock-faced man whose erect carriage made him seem taller than he actually was. . . . Dan had over fifty items he must personally observe . . . he was well aware that many of them were potential murderers.

The years had taught Dan Roman the criminal histories of the mechanical contrivances; he knew only too well how the most innocent of them might combine with circumstance to kill. . . .

Looking up at the big ship . . . Dan stood with his feet wide

LYDIA who was as low as high society could get!

CHILDS a wealthy collector—of other men's wives!

MAY strictly a night-time woman!

NELL still burning with honeymoon fever!

SALLY who lived in a world of whistles!

DAN who had used up his nine lives, and was starting on ten!

THE HIGH AND THE MIGHTY by ERNEST K. GANN

Dan shares a lighthearted moment with Ken Childs, the "wealthy collector of other people's wives."

apart and his arms folded across his chest . . . his only thoughts for the moment were of the ship before him. It was really far more than a machine. It was a whole era which he had helped create. . . .

Now once more, he was a part of it—and in a way that was laughable. . . .

And how much remained of the old Dan Roman besides the inevitable suspended look—the appearance of not really belonging anywhere, a vague, unsettled look, acquired in time by all professional pilots? . . .

The slight limp came from the accident, and so that could not be considered pure deterioration. Glasses were easier for reading, but the depth perception . . . was just as good as ever. Heart, according to the last physical, remarkably sound. . . .

Dan Roman—not quite yet a relic.

Sad Dan, who didn't know when to quit.

The lean-faced "Skipper" is Captain Sullivan (Robert Stack). He is cool, taciturn, and full of self-belief. He is like all pilots, but he lacks experience and, in spite of his many hours of flying, silently battles his own irrational fears that he might not be able to handle a crisis. Fear breeds caution in him. He resents Roman and thinks his copilot might guess at his low confidence; the older man makes him feel like an amateur. Sullivan visibly shakes the concern off and asks the weather forecaster if there are any ships near the flight path. His is told there are two Coast Guard cutters anchored at sea, serving as transmitting stations, and a couple of liners but nothing else.

Hobie Wheeler (William Campbell) is the third pilot, a brash twenty-two-year-old. He is about to learn that flying can get rough. He worships Captain Sullivan and also resents Dan being foisted on them: "He should be left to graze in the pasture."

Leonard Wilby (Wally Brown) is the navigator. He is almost as old as Dan. He loves just two things, his ability to navigate and his faithless, drunken wife, Susie. She had once called him "a miserable bowl of prune whip, surrounded by gray hairs," but still he loved her.

Spalding (Doe Avedon) is the vibrant stewardess. After four months with the company, she is friendly and efficient and laughingly rejects the amorous attention of Wheeler.

Behind the flight deck the passengers begin to stow their coats and bags before taking their places. Spalding moves amongst them and helps them settle. Sullivan doesn't worry about his passengers when Spalding is around. She is good at her job.

Lydia and Howard Rice (Laraine Day and John Howard) are returning to the mainland to get a divorce. Lydia is cold and aloof and very rich. Howard, feeling like a kept man, wants to go off to prospect for gold so he can make something of himself. They certainly no longer want the same things. They quarrel as usual. Lydia petulantly nags her husband. Howard's eyes are haunted by the knowledge of failure. He does not want divorce.

The Josephs, Ed (Phil Harris) and "The Mrs." (Ann Doran), are a couple of small-towners who had saved for years for their trip to Hawaii. Professor Don Flaherty (Paul Kelly) is a physicist obsessed with and traumatized by his role in developing weapons of mass destruction. He sits down and promptly pulls out a bottle of whiskey.

Ken Childs (David Brian) is a handsome bachelor, a "wealthy collector of other people's wives." Spalding stops to talk to him. The flight agent back in Honolulu has warned her he is an influential company stock holder and he will expect extra attention from her. He exudes carefree confidence.

Gustave Pardee (Robert Newton) is a theatrical producer and terrified of flying, and his wife Lillian (Julie Bishop) is struggling to maintain a glittering life and marriage. She is desperately unhappy and bitter. Spalding tries to

Wellman and Wayne; who is directing whom?

reassure Gustave. Lillian seems amused by his fear. There is a hint of malice about her.

Frank Briscoe (Paul Fix) is a dying invalid in constant pain but trying to live out his life as best he can. As she walks back toward the galley, Spalding hears a faint chiming coming from his vest and gasps with delight when she sees him take out a small gold watch. Somehow she seems to know he is going to die and that he wants to give her the watch. She knows her acceptance will make him happy and refusal would embarrass him, so she promises to take care of it.

Jose Locota (John Qualen) is an Italian-born fisherman returning home from a business trip. "He falls into the 'nobody' category," according to the flight agent at the boarding gate.

Toby Field (Michael Wellman) is a bored four-year-old catching the plane to return to his mother after his vacation with his estranged dad.

The Bucks, Milo (John Smith) and Nell (Karen Sharpe), are in-love honeymooners returning home.

The other passengers include a host of beautiful women. Dorothy Chen (Joy Kim) is a shy Korean girl going to school in America. Sally McKee (Jan Sterling) is afraid to go back to America to meet a man she's never seen but who had fallen in love with a picture of her taken six years before when she had been young and beautiful. Sullivan notices her tragic eyes and pancake makeup. She has a furtive manner as she asks the captain if she can slip out of the door used by the crew when the plane lands. She tells him there is a man waiting that she does not want to meet. She has changed her mind and is scared.

May Holst (Claire Trevor) is the proverbial loose woman with a heart of gold, who for fifteen years had happily loved and had an affair with a married man. He had died suddenly, leaving her very lonely, and she now hides her desire for affection behind cynical quips. Childs has already noticed her, and she smiles coyly back across the aisle at him.

A mysterious last-minute traveler, Humphrey Agnew (Sidney Blackmer), had arrived at the ticket office and demanded a flight on the same plane as Kenneth Childs. He carries a black scowl on his face and murder in his heart. He watches Spalding intently, oddly.

Up front, Sullivan hands over to Roman, who calmly checks the instruments. They are all functioning normally. Leonard stretches out and Hobie talks casually to the Coast Guard cutter below. The plane wings its way toward its destination through a darkening sky, while in the cabin Lydia quarrels violently with her husband.

Spalding is the first to sense the few unexpected vibrations that might suggest trouble when she glances at her shaky reflection in the washroom mirror. Dan also notices something. Later, as Spalding prepares coffee, she is startled as the tray suddenly slides away from her. Captain Sullivan offers to take the controls back. He also senses trouble.

As the personal dramas have begun to unfold, so the DC-4 develops a series of small mechanical problems about seven hours from San Francisco.

Then there it is. A sudden violent jolt. Dan and Sullivan stare at the instrument panel. Nothing unusual there. Spalding bursts in to report the vibrations. Sullivan glances out of the cockpit window and murmurs, "I could swear it's the number-one engine, but it's running perfectly."

"Maybe there's something wrong with the tail," Leonard suggests.

Sullivan orders Roman to go and check the tail cone and Wheeler to report the vibrations to San Francisco but not to declare an emergency yet. Nervous tension is building, and Roman watches Sullivan curiously as he gets up. He has instinctively recognized the signs of fear. There is no vibration in the tail cone. Roman is sure the trouble is elsewhere, up front, where he felt the first jolt. He limps back down the aisle toward the flight deck.

Childs, a veteran of many flights, also suspects something has happened with the plane. He becomes slightly stressed. Jose Locota notices Agnew, brooding and sinister, pacing the aisle, staring aggressively at Childs. Suddenly Agnew pounces

Searching for trouble.

and accuses Childs of wife stealing and confronts him with a gun. Childs jumps to his feet. As the other passengers rush to Childs's rescue, there is a burst of noise and the plane lurches violently.

On the flight deck there is now intense, noisy vibration. One of the engines is ablaze and has been shaken loose to dangle precariously from the wing. Flying speed and altitude are lost suddenly as precious gasoline leaks away into the night. Hobie reaches across Sullivan to pull the valve that releases carbon dioxide into the area around the number-one engine. His action douses the fire.

"Get on the radio! Tell San Francisco!" Sullivan ordered. His voice returned momentarily to normal, yet he seemed physically paralyzed. . . .

All the youthful bounce had left Hobie . . . his carefully groomed hair was no longer so . . . somehow he had lost co-ordination as he worked the radios. . . .

Only Dan Roman, who stood between them, seemed the same, although the easy, rather sad little smile . . . was no longer on his lips . . . he was entirely calm, almost statuesque.

"Are you going to declare an emergency?" asks one of the crew of Trans-Orient-Pacific Airlines, Flight 420.

Frantic calls fail to raise San Francisco. Roman sucks hard on his cigarette. He isn't whistling anymore. His mouth is dry. Down below, a merchant ship's radio operator (Pedro Gonzales Gonzales) is tuned to the airline frequency on his ham radio and establishes the first contact.

He links the aircraft to the Coast Guard, and the sea-air rescue unit swings into immediate action. Air traffic control clears the air of all planes below Sullivan. Panic breaks out amongst the passengers. The plane has passed the point of no return, and it must continue eastward or ditch. Sullivan is undecided; but feels it would be safest to ditch the plane, saying, "We're going into the drink."

> His strong hands made a caressing movement around the control wheel and he was suddenly aware that this previously ordinary machine at his command had become a precious unit which he hated to damage. If only he could get hold of himself!
> All the doubts and illusions that had been gnawing at his courage for months, the haunting fear of failure or of mistakes made when they should not be made . . . were resolved. He was afraid but he no longer cringed. . . .

Dan is forced to take control when Sullivan freezes.

"Hold on to me! Grab me around the waist!"

Then Sullivan changes his mind because the sea is rough and it is nighttime. He dithers and finally orders the passengers to prepare for a wet landing. He becomes hysterical, cracking under the pressure, and Dan is forced to take over command.

Dan explains the situation to the passengers. He is calm but realistic about their chances. He tells them the truth. He orders cargo and baggage to be thrown out to lighten the ship. It is unlikely the now-scant gasoline will hold out, but Dan believes they have a chance.

The peril they are in brings about changes in them all. From his copilot's stubborn determination, Sullivan gains new courage, as do the passengers whose lives seem to take a turn for the better as they each stare long and hard at their own mortality. The terrified Pardee suddenly becomes calm and assertive, the would-be murderer Agnew becomes prostrate with fear, McKee and Holst seem to be carefree, and Lydia, impressed by her husband's quiet strength, decides against divorce—maybe she does love him after all.

Roman's quiet confidence may reassure others—he never acknowledges he has given up hope himself—but he is perfectly well aware that none of them are likely to survive.

The Coast Guard plane, flying blind in the storm, eventually locates the stricken ship and turns to convoy it in. Everyone prepares for a crash landing. Sullivan still plans to ditch. Dan worries about Sullivan's decision. If he were captain he would try to reach the San Francisco airport. He knows fuel gauges are not always accurate. Dan gives his advice and grabs for the controls as Sullivan freezes, telling the captain, "Hang on and *fly*, man."

Sullivan's eyes brighten and he sets about the struggle of bringing the plane in. Barely clearing the San Francisco hills, he brings the plane down at the airport—a routine landing. He turns toward Dan Roman. His fear has gone. He's cured. And a tired old has-been who called him a yellow son of a bitch has made him whole again.

"Now I lay me down to sleep," sighs a relieved Dan.

The plane taxis up to the lighted airport, and the passengers begin to disembark. As the crowd disperses, Garfield waits to talk to Sullivan and Roman. His eyes are warm with affection for Dan as he approaches wearily, the limp pronounced as he avoids the puddles on the tarmac.

"Get a good night's sleep, Dan. We'll get together soon."

"Sure, chum."

Dan walks away to his lonely room, whistling into the dark.

"So long, you ancient pelican."

There wasn't much to spare.

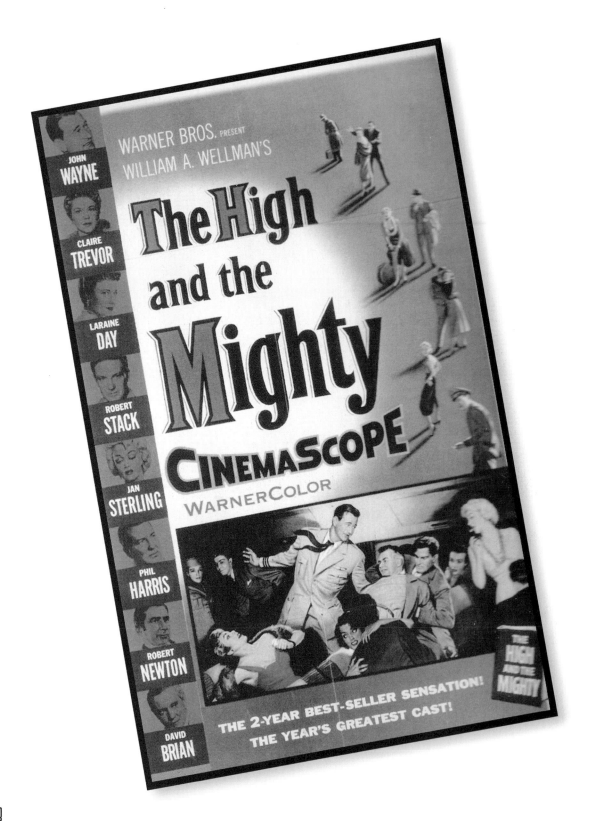

CHAPTER 6
Production Notes for
The High and the Mighty

John Wayne as Dan Roman, Director William Wellman, and Assistant Director Andrew McLaglen discuss business on the soundstage.

● ● ●

LOCATION

Faithfully based on a best-selling novel by Ernest K. Gann, *The High and the Mighty*, the fifth Wayne-Fellows production, was shot mostly on the Goldwyn lot and Warners soundstages in Hollywood from November 25, 1953, to January 11, 1954. Some minor location work was done in Hawaii, and scenes were shot at the Royal Hawaiian Hotel, Waikiki Beach, and at the airport. After being given production code clearance of the final script by Joseph Breen, location players were dispatched to San Francisco to be photographed at Fisherman's Wharf, the Coast Guard station and the Oakland airport. Breen had already notified Wayne-Fellows of certain required changes: "Sally, in appearance, will not be suggestive of a prostitute," "May Holst must not come across as a mistress, her relationship must be clarified in an acceptable manner," "It will not be possible for May to reveal several inches of bare leg above her garter. Something of a less suggestive nature should be substituted."

Throughout filming, Coast Guard Lieutenant Commander Robert C. Cannom acted as technical advisor. Also on location, permission was authorized by the government for Wayne's crew to film the flight of a guided missile at the U.S. Naval Testing Station at Inyokern. No special firing was staged for the company, but William Clothier was permitted to film a regular test. When told the missile would be traveling over 1,000 miles per hour, he asked, "How can I photograph that?"

Frozen with fear, pilot Sullivan allows Dan to snatch the controls and save the flight from ditching.

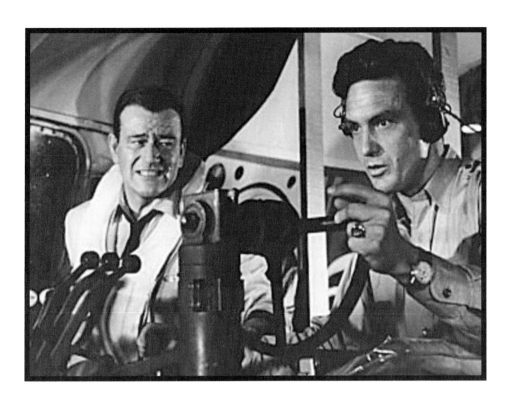

Calmer, Sullivan resumes control.

The expert quipped, "You might fasten your camera to another rocket!"

The High and the Mighty gave the public the first picture of the Coast Guard's air-sea rescue unit in action. Both planes and ships of the guard are shown, tracking down the crippled passenger plane and convoying it to safety.

Wellman's second unit cameraman, detailed to fly the camera plane into a storm, had a problem with unseasonably sedate weather and had to fly over 10,000 miles to complete his mission.

Budgeted at $1,320,000, the motion picture was completed at a negative cost of $1,465,000 on its exact schedule of thirty-four days. Wayne received a salary of $175,000 and a hefty percentage of the profits. Wellman was paid $100,000 and also a percentage of the profits. The film earned total rentals of $8.5 million on a domestic box-office gross of $15,500,000. Distinguished by one of the finest groups of screen personalities ever assembled on a single soundstage, the movie was destined to become one of the ten biggest hits of the year.

The spectacular, filmed in WarnerColor, was Duke's first movie attempt in CinemaScope.

THE CAST

Casting the film with twenty-two top players had proved a nightmare for Wayne-Fellows and Wellman. *The High and the Mighty* was the first in a long series of Hollywood disaster movies that hosted a large cast of troubled characters, and since the movie largely concentrates on human emotion, with a script that explores crisis and its effects on the individual passengers, the film had no real need of a central star character. A number of big-name stars including Joan Crawford, Ida Lupino, Barbara Stanwyck, Ginger Rogers, and Dorothy McGuire, turned Wayne-Fellows down; possibly the individual parts didn't appear big enough. Many stars judged a job purely on the number of pages of dialogue they were being offered. Wellman later admitted he was discouraged by the attitude, saying some had been insulted to be offered roles! Production delay was caused, and eventually, Wayne decided not to bother about big stars: "I decided instead to get competent, fine actors and actresses."

He and Wellman hired Claire Trevor, Laraine Day, Robert Stack, Jan Sterling, Phil Harris, Robert Newton, David Brian, Paul Kelly, Sidney Blackmer, and Julie Bishop—not a giant among them, but Wellman still commented that he believed Trevor was the greatest actress of her day. The final selection of stars all had to be available at the same time. John Wayne took time out from his divorce hearing to personally sign Robert Stack to his company. Wayne had originally cast Robert Cummings as the pilot because he could actually fly a plane. But Wellman preferred Stack and had casting right. "With Duke, you were what you were," Stack said. "In other words, the performance factor to him was less important than getting some guy that really knew how to fly a plane." While Wayne accepted Stack, it did make for a "hairy few days," according to the actor.

Almost everyone made suggestions as to casting, and Louella Parsons claimed she helped Wayne choose Jan Sterling to play the controversial role of shady Sally McKee. In one scene McKee has to remove all her makeup and even Wellman himself warned the star it would prove difficult for her; three other stars, including Stanwyck, had already rejected the part, "But I grabbed it. I'm gunning for a career that's going to last, and if McKee's big moment came when she looked ugliest, so what? How long can a girl depend upon glamour?"

Laraine Day had also gone out of her way for a part and got her agent to put pressure on Wellman. She wanted the Jan Sterling role, but considered herself lucky to be in the picture at all. She had no idea why some of the big actresses had turned their offers down: "Some of those actresses weren't getting good roles then. Wellman was wonderful to me. He had a sort of wicked reputation. But his son, [now a producer], played the little boy in it, so Wellman always quit shooting at 5:30 and was home for dinner by six. I found him to be very pleasant. I think he may have picked on Robert Stack, a very emotional character."

A surprise casting was that of Phil Harris, known largely for comedy radio, his TV work, and also as a band leader, for the part of Ed Joseph. Wayne-Fellows also introduced three newcomers, recently placed under contract, two of whom made their first screen appearance. Doe Avedon was called up from the stage after her actor husband was killed in an automobile crash. Cast as Spalding, she has more screen time than anyone else, appearing in every scene. Wayne anticipated she would make a big impact on movie-goers. Avedon became a star for Wayne despite herself. When interviewed she said that all she wanted was to be an everyday girl and that she had steadfastly refused all offers of work until she suddenly found herself widowed. She had then turned to Charlie Feldman for help, and he arranged for her to test for *The High and the Mighty*.

The picture's other debut performers are Karen Sharpe, appearing as honeymooner Nell Buck, and the remarkably efficient Michael Wellman, the little boy on the plane who sleeps innocently throughout all the action, a talisman that everything will come out all right in the end. The four-year-old son of the director earned $350 a week for his maiden acting debut, and Wellman said, "Mike is the greatest actor I have used in my whole life. I'd say, 'Alright, Mike, you go into your spot now and you go to sleep.' He said, 'Do you want me to go to sleep or do you want me to "play" sleep?' He went to sleep, and I'd shoot all around him. At lunchtime we had to waken him. He had a lot of fun."

Mike's presence in the film was penciled into the script at a late stage, but he enabled John Wayne's character to show, in a few wordless scenes, a deep vein of tenderness. It is also his sleepy presence on board that keeps Dan Roman's insistence on landing the stricken plane from being an act of reckless bravado. He wants the boy to wake up in San Francisco and not know anything unusual had happened.

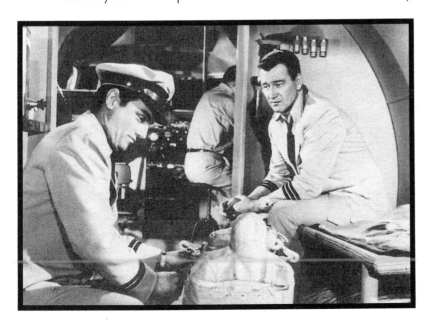

Hobie puts Dan down for being a has-been, but William Campbell admitted, "I was in such awe of John Wayne that I found it difficult to work with him."

Wellman had lined up Spencer Tracy for the part of Dan Roman: "We had lunch and shook on the deal." Tracy later pulled out with just days to spare. Lionel Barrymore and Keenan Wynn were also reputedly to be loaned to Wayne-Fellows by Metro, but they were suddenly withdrawn with no reason being given. It was reportedly because a clause in the contract stated the film could be sold to TV later.

Part of the problem was Wellman himself; his tough reputation was famed, and he was known in the business for not pulling punches. A big part was also the plot itself. Since an entire planeload of passengers had to spend day after day, week after week simply strapped in their seats, the work was destined to become tedious for all concerned. "Everybody whose ear was in camera range had to sit there," Claire Trevor, who was happy to escape sordid roles, remembered. "It was a dreary picture to make."

It was monotonously dull work, and Laraine Day said, "That was all there was to the set, day after day. The seats were all removable. They took out sections so the camera could move in. Of course there was no top to the plane." She solved the problem of boredom by doing cryptograms with John Howard. Ann Doran and Phil Harris, playing a husband and wife on their second honeymoon, remained in character and, according to Doran, "Got a little silly." To add to the discomfort, the weather turned cold and the soundstage wasn't heated properly. Doran said, "Most of us sitting in the plane were sick."

Laraine Day as Lydia Rice.

Andrew McLaglen remembered Wellman as the best-prepared director he had ever met but agreed he was also a disciplinarian who could browbeat his actors. Friends who had worked with Wellman warned Tracy that he was in for an ego-bruising experience and the actor decided to back out. He told Wellman however that he thought the script was "lousy." Wellman said, "He changed his mind. Didn't think the role was good enough for him, I guess."

With Tracy's departure, Jack Warner threatened to pull Warner Bros. out of the distribution deal, and the picture gradually edged its way toward the shelf. Wayne was left with no alternative but to take the part of Dan Roman himself at the last minute. Although he worried that the role might be too much of a departure from his usual persona, calling it a "walk-on part," Dan Roman is John Stryker in a commercial pilot uniform—cool, competent, fearless, a man of few words who acts rather than talks. Laraine Day said, "John Wayne probably didn't want to be in the picture. It wasn't his type of thing, but I guess he couldn't get another actor. I can see where he wouldn't want to do it, but it turned out to be one of the best pictures that year."

Unless Duke agreed to star in the movie, Jack L. Warner threatened to pull out of the distribution deal.

Since his performance took place mainly in the cockpit, he didn't work with the planeload of actors. But he was on set most of the time as producer. "I had a row with Duke," Wellman said. "I made three pictures with him . . . and in *The High and the Mighty* he suddenly wanted to become a director." In front of the entire crew Wellman told him, "Look, you come back here behind the camera and do my job, and you're going to be just as ridiculous doing it as I would be out there with that screwy voice of yours and that fairy walk and being Duke Wayne." Wayne offered no more interference.

"With all of Bill Wellman's bad language and ripping around, he knew how to get the performances he wanted," Ann Doran said. "Sometimes it was because he yelled at people; he bawled them out, he belittled them, and they showed him by giving a superb performance. Other times he was so nice and so sweet and so understanding that you exploded all over. That's what he did with me to get me to cry. I had such a dreadful cold when we got to the close-up that I couldn't see. Somehow he knew how to approach each one of us and get the thing he wanted. Wayne realized that no matter what he played, he had to be John Wayne. That was his salable point. The only argument he had with Wellman over his performance was when Bill suggested something that was inconsistent with the John Wayne persona. Bill always saw his point."

Robert Stack grew fascinated with the way Wayne could say lines out loud, as they were written, but still make them sound like John Wayne saying them. "I'd get behind a flat and listen to his reading of the dialogue," Stack said, "and I'd think, 'Man, that's really not very good.' And for radio it wasn't very good. But the minute

Robert Stack as Captain Sullivan. "Without a good part an actor is dead," said Stack. His success in The High and the Mighty made him a top star.

Claire Trevor, a John Wayne favorite leading lady, played May Holst.

you saw that great American face up there on the screen, it didn't matter. He could have been talking Esperanto and nobody would give a damn!"

In fact, Day recalled that Wayne himself didn't really have much to do around the set except "be John Wayne. When you played a scene with him, you were playing it with the John Wayne everybody loved. He was a big guy. He called me his 'little Mormon.' There was never anyone else like him. He deserved every bit of success, and he handled it so beautifully." She said that his performance in *The High and the Mighty* could not be criticized.

Wayne's girlfriend, Pilar Palette, sat on the set most of the time throughout shooting. "She was delightful," Day recalled, "very shy, and she had none of the obvious attributes of an actress. She seemed sort of in a shell." Others found Palette aloof and attributed her standoffish behavior to her aristocratic South American background. In truth she was sensitive about her lack of formal education and limited command of English, yet she found living in the big, isolated house in Encino lonely. "I always felt I was in the way when I went to watch Duke shoot," she said. "They would put a chair out for me, and then I'd have to move because I was in the way of the cables. I found it all pretty boring and not really as glamorous as I'd thought." Eventually Palette began playing tennis at Robert Stack's house to while away the lonely hours.

Day confessed, "I loved working with Duke. We did lots of gags like taking people's keys and marking them up, 'If found, return to John Wayne. REWARD.' All of a sudden he is being plagued by people coming to the studio and presenting these keys and waiting for their reward. He took it all good-naturedly." The director, long known as "Wild Bill," found himself the butt of one of Wayne's jokes when he found "Sweet William" painted on the back of his chair. Day said, "Still, he had the whole set jumping and was sweet for whole minutes at a time."

Wellman found the CinemaScope camera bulky and unwieldy, especially when composing scenes, but he raved about the super widescreen effect. Instead of scanning a scene with a moving lens, he found it easier to station the CinemaScope camera in one place and let the actors move in and out of the picture, almost a complete reversion to the cinematic technique of the silent era. Fortunately *The High and the Mighty* set consisted of little more than the full interior of a cramped cockpit and passenger cabin of a DC-4 aircraft, and Wellman did not need to employ the same variety of cinematic techniques he used in action pictures. At the end of filming, he had a newfound respect for the skill of cameraman William Clothier.

The director never went through many takes, and he was working with some very good, professional stars. He usually did no more than three takes of any scene on the picture. Because the camera lens brought people's faces up close, he couldn't cut as often as normal.

Archie Stout, freshly teamed up again with William Wellman, loved working on

The High and the Mighty, "Once again, it was a big challenge from start to finish. There were problems with color contrasts and lighting. This was my first film in Cinema-Scope. We were filming with a wide-angle lens in the confines of a fifty-foot cabin for 80 percent of the picture. I did everything a cameraman should not do."

William Campbell, who starred as Hobie Wheeler, remembered:

I was in such awe of John Wayne that I found it difficult to work with him. Can't begin to tell you what it was like to work with him in *The High and the Mighty*. It was frightening, yet unbelievably satisfying. He was sensitive to how other people felt. Once you were on the picture with him, he took you in. Still, at the same time I'm sure he recognized how powerful he really was.

It was easy to see he adored working. It was more than just a job to be done. On occasion he was prone to say to Wellman, "I wouldn't have said that." He would hand lines to different people. People joked about his acting. But I've watched him in everything. He had sense.

We were physically close for hours at a time. In one scene with him I really had great fears and a number of sleepless nights. In it I'm putting him down for being old. I'm telling him to keep his mouth shut. I'm telling him with his history who the hell is he to be suggesting anything . . . I thought to myself, *Jesus Christ, I'm going to be tongue-lashing John Wayne*. And we did it in very close quarters. It just went phenomenally well. He listened to what I was saying, reacted to what was going on. When Wayne worked with you, he never would be, or could be, threatened by any other actor, unlike some others.

Some actors weave a scene to make their character more important. Wayne never, ever did that. He knew what he was doing, always knew his lines, was professional. He had a problem in that he was so big, overpowering. It didn't matter who had the authority in a scene; Wayne was always bigger. That's why he always seemed so comfortable lounging in the background, letting others have all the good lines. Inevitably the eye is drawn to him. He has the attention, whatever else is going on.

Walter Reed recalls appearing with Wayne in *The High and the Mighty*:

I was the guy who put the small boy on the plane. Wellman's son Mike played my son in the picture. He sleeps all

William Campbell as Hobie Wheeler.

through the picture.

I had been up for a bigger part. Andy McLaglen had me come to Wellman's home to have me interviewed. Since Duke was producing the picture, I went there also and waited outside Bob Fellows's office. I heard him say, "Walter Reed! I don't want some stock boy doing this part." He talked Wellman out of using me. Wellman gave me the smaller part.

So after I got through with the scene, Wayne comes over and says, "Wellman's really mad." I asked him why. Duke said, "He really liked you in the scene and why did he let that jerk talk him out of using Walter Reed?"

Warner Brothers prepared a trailer made by John Wayne for the film, in which Duke said, "Must seem kinda funny to see me on the screen with a book in my hand instead of a gun, but when you're hunting for what makes a great motion picture entertainment, here's where you begin, with a story. And a good story is only as strong as its characters and only as interesting as the things they do. *The High and the Mighty* is about people; all kinds, good, bad, strong and weak, brave ones and cowards, tossed together on an adventure that spans three thousand miles of ocean. They're people you won't forget.

"Oh yeah, an' I almost forgot. I'm in it too."

While its plot may have been somewhat synthetic, haphazardly tossing all kinds of people together, the special effects and performances make for an engaging film in which, as usual, Wayne gave of his best.

MUSIC AND WHISTLING

Faced with declining box office returns, Hollywood producers had learned that a title song could be an effective way to publicize current movies. The theme Dimitri Tiomkin composed for *The High and the Mighty* soared to the top of the Hit Parade and remained there for many weeks, contributing greatly to the movie's popularity.

The whistling, a forty-five-second chorus and a twenty-second take in the film, was recorded for Wayne by Muzzy Marcellino.

Despite its popularity, the theme tune was ruled out of Academy Award consideration for a while because it was whistled rather than sung. The Academy changed its mind late in December 1954, making arrangements for it to be nominated for an Oscar. The song lyrics, performed by a choir, had been heard at the fade-out in original showings of the movie. But before its original release the last sixty seconds of the picture were cut, tightening the running time. After the number made the Hit Parade, Tiomkin launched sheet music, and lyrics were added by Ned Washington, it was restored to the film, giving it last-minute eligibility for Best Song. For the first time in Academy history, a studio pinned its hopes on a special second-run showing at the Picfair Theatre since Academy rules stipulated that any eligible film had to be exhibited in Los Angeles for a one-week run which must begin prior to December 31.

All Hollywood got behind Tiomkin in his bid for recognition, and Jack Moffitt wrote in *The Hollywood Reporter* in September 1954, "Dimitri has no big organization to beat the tubs for him when the halos are being fitted by the Academy. But he has a record of solid accomplishment. . . . His score for *The High and the Mighty* did just about everything that music could do for a picture. . . . It got out and sold the picture. That lonely, haunting, whistled refrain summed up, as no spoken words ever could, the things that were going on in the heart and soul of the John Wayne character. Sad and despairing, it was, at the same time, persevering. That wistfully romantic little tune, associated with the picture's title, made millions of people buy tickets." At the Academy Awards *The High and the Mighty* won for Tiomkin's score but not for Best Song, even though a doctored version of the picture with an added vocal was screened for a week in L.A. to qualify it for the Oscars. The theme also revived the whistling habit in America. In a national survey of disc jockeys in 1955, the song was voted the "most whistleable tune."

In 1958 Tiomkin was sued by Leon Navarro in a plagiarism suit over the song. A unanimous decision by a New York Supreme Court found in favor of Tiomkin after hearing singing lawyers, pianos, and tape recordings and watching the film itself. Navarro had sued Tiomkin, Ned Washington, Warner Bros., Witmark Music, and

Ralph Dawson, editor.

Dimitri Tiomkin, music.

Wayne-Fellows for $100,000 each, claiming the theme was stolen from one of his tunes, "Enchanted Cello." Theme tune detective Sigmund Spaeth laughed at the trial. "Only one note, a B-flat, appears in the same place in both songs!" That note was expensively argued about in court for two days.

Fellows had had minor problems with music throughout production. When John Qualen played one of his own untitled compositions on the harmonica for a scene as requested by Wellman, the multi Academy Award–winning editor Ralph Dawson said it sounded like a piece that had been aired by CBS in the TV series *Danger*. Copies and transcripts of the show had to be tracked down, and in early May 1954 the company was no nearer learning if they could include the song in the picture. Eventually Wayne himself decided the music was not even similar. He called Ralph a brilliant man, saying that he had achieved as tight a print as ever, but that he wanted to "eat" him out about the delay and fuss he had caused over nothing.

Wayne-Fellows also had to pay handsomely to include the Coast Guard song "Semper Paratus" in the film. Fellows wrote to the Coast Guard Liaison Office, "We included the song as a goodwill gesture on our part. It was not necessary to the picture. This song is published through arrangement with the Coast Guard by Sam Fox Publishing Company of the Music Publisher's Protective Association. They are quoting us a price of $1,000 for its use in the picture."

WARDROBE AND PROPS

Gwen Wakeling, wardrobe designer, admitted she had her simplest assignment, all the female leads having only one costume each. Some of her original designs for the movie, particularly those for Joy Kim, are spectacular and can still be viewed at the Academy of Motion Picture Arts and Sciences. On the other hand, Carl Walker, who assembled the men's wardrobe said he used around 10,000 separate items for the various players.

Patrick Wayne was assistant prop man during his school break.

PREMIERE—MAY 27, 1954

Wayne was worried about the film and didn't like what he saw of his own performance in the rushes. Wellman loved it. "Do you mean to tell me you don't think you were good in that?" he asked incredulously. "What's wrong with it? Wayne says, 'Well, he never had a love story.' And I said, 'He had the greatest love story that had ever been written. No one ever saw you with your wife, no one ever saw your kid. All they saw was the half-burned-up old bear that was taken out of the wreck, and you're a lonesome, attractive, wonderful man. You couldn't ask for anything better.'"

A few weeks before its release, Wellman told a reporter, "Oh, we argue like hell. Wayne thinks his performance is lousy, and I think he's crazy. It turned out to be a great part for him, and it would have been great for Tracy. To hell with those other big stars. They think they know so much!" It turned out that Wellman was right.

The world premiere was held at the Egyptian Theatre in Hollywood on May 27, 1954. Duke attended with Pilar Palette although they remained unmarried pending his divorce. Hollywood Boulevard spilled over with old-time glamour. The Egyptian canopy sparkled with floral decorations, waterfalls, spotlights, and a 150-foot red carpet, making it the biggest premiere of the year. Up to four thousand fans turned out to cheer the 150 attending top Hollywood stars. (Later, to accommodate record-breaking crowds outside theaters all over the country, there were extended runs, and Hollywood ran the film in two theaters simultaneously.)

Wayne acted as master of ceremonies for radio and a half-hour television special, assisted arriving celebrities and personally introduced his fellow cast members. He also autographed a huge replica of Gann's book jacket.

Wayne was encouraged enough by the reception of his film that night to predict a resurgence in the motion picture industry, if only by bringing back extravagant productions and lavish premieres. *The High and the Mighty* proved a huge commercial success. It was a smash hit and huge moneymaker for Wayne-Fellows. Duke seemed to be taken by surprise by the interest in his movie but commented, "With the wide screen and new color techniques, Hollywood is now turning with new confidence to more magnificent costuming and sets. There is no doubt about the demand for good pictures in whatever dimension."

The trade papers lavished praise on the film. Most importantly *The Hollywood Reporter* commented, "It gives the public something it cannot get on television. It makes a trip to the movies a big event for any family, and it restores to the screen a place of importance."

The movie was nominated for six Academy Awards, more than any other John Wayne film except *Stagecoach*, *The Quiet Man*, and *The Alamo*.

With the completion of *The High and the Mighty*, Wayne formally bought out Robert Fellows's interest in their production unit and renamed the company Batjac.

Both Wellman and McLaglen won congratulations for Directorial Achievement by the Screen Directors Guild. Apart from Dimitri Tiomkin's 1954 Academy Award for music (scoring, dramatic or comedy picture), several other cast and crew members were also nominated: supporting actress, Jan Sterling and Claire Trevor; directing, William Wellman; film editing, Ralph Dawson; music (song) *The High and the Mighty* (Music by Dimitri Tiomkin and lyrics by Ned Washington).

Wayne introduces Academy Award winner Dimitri Tiomkin and newcomer Karen Sharpe to the crowds outside the Egyptian Theatre.

Los Angeles Examiner—May 28, 1954
by Dorothy Manners

They came, they saw—they gasped!

Wayne turns in the finest performance of his career. He has a scene telling the passengers of the trouble they're in for that has seldom been topped for emotional restraint.

The New York Times—July 1, 1954
by Bosley Crowther

William A. Wellman directs it with the vigor and snap he's always shown. . . . Of the four crewmen, John Wayne makes the best show as a veteran pilot, second in command, who has the coolness and courage to knock some clear sense into the muddled head of the captain.

Variety—May 26, 1954

It is a class drama, blended with mass appeal into a well-rounded show that can catch on with most any audience. A definite ticket-selling asset is the name of John Wayne. Hearty grosses should be the rule.

The Motion Picture Guide

A stirring and often frightening production . . . providing a socko story and wonderful characters. . . . One of the most memorable film scores ever. . . . Wayne's performance . . . was outstanding.

The Motion Picture Herald—May 29, 1954
by James D. Ivers

Warner Brothers here present a mighty motion picture that bears every happy auspice of being a production that the public will long remember as superb entertainment and the industry as a box office giant. It is an event in the history of the screen as a story-telling medium such as happens all too rarely in spite of Hollywood's best efforts when story, cast, direction, cinematography, editing and all the technical elements of a film drama combine to narrate a tale certain to grip any audience and to send them away at happy at its end.

Los Angeles Times—May 28, 1954
by Edwin Schallert

An enormously vital picture, amazingly associated with life's panorama today, and thus filled with a rare kind of tingling excitement, especially for a modern air-minded public.

It was no wonder that the premier was voted by insiders as an event to recall the great gala days of the silent films.

The Examiner—May 1954

This Wayne-Fellows production shows how great a picture can be.

On seeing this picture, one important fact emerged. Bob Stack has been given the opportunity to act. He is no newcomer to movies but it is not often that he has had the opportunity to play so vital a part and be successful . . . Stack will attract so much attention through this great film that at last he will have achieved stardom and offers will flow in.

Saturday Review Syndicate
by John Barkham

Will keep you sitting on the edge of your chair in sheer suspense . . . don't miss it.

San Francisco Chronicle
by Joseph Henry Jackson

Wonderfully done . . . a story that gives you no time to catch your breath.

To-Days Cinema, September 2, 1954
by MMW

Close and careful direction has been needed to keep the many story-threads from becoming entangled, and here William Wellman has succeeded admirably. . . . Action and dialogue have each the right emphasis. . . . John Wayne plays with real authority. A penetrating human drama; flying thrills; outstanding star appeal.

LA Times—October 7, 1954,
by Richard Griffin

The High and the Mighty opened in New York last week and was dubbed "The Grand Hotel of the Sky." Several critics objected to the superficiality of the human types gathered together. One reviewer states, "All are fabricated characters—and that is the way they are played."

Saturday Review—July 3, 1954
by Lee Rogow

It is an unbelievably long trip. The one I liked was John Qualen . . . because he seemed to be the only person on the plane who just wanted to get to San Francisco.

Hollywood Reporter—June 24, 1954
by Jack Moffitt

The High and the Mighty proves that Hollywood may profit by having successful authors participate in the dramatization of their own works. The public that thrilled to his printed pages will not feel cheated when it goes to the theatre, for there, compressed in two and a half hours of running time, it will find all the merits of the book.

There are secondary scenes written with more skill and beauty in this picture than the big scenes in most pictures.

Cue—July 3, 1954

A successful combination of tight script, masterful direction and production, skillful editing . . . plus well-nigh perfect performances by a distinguished multi-star cast.

Fortnight—June 2, 1954

This drama wields strong emotional power in its tension-filled chronicle of impending air tragedy. . . . It is dissipated, however, by the extreme length of its proceedings, which seems almost full flight time Honolulu–San Francisco.

LA Times—June 6th, 1954

I don't know whether the picture starring John Wayne truly merits the adjective *great*; let us say, rather it is the kind of rattling good movie for which, when the industry was really rolling, we used to crowd the theatres automatically every couple of weeks.

Daily News—Los Angeles, May 28, 1954,
by Howard McClay

Ranks with some of the greatest films ever produced by Hollywood. . . .

This whopping screen version of Ernest K. Gann's bestseller retains all the drama and suspense that made the author's novel a national success.

Although Wayne draws top billing, he does not rule the footage, yet his appearance is strong throughout.

Paul Fix, Pedro Gonzales Gonzales (above, right), and Joy Kim.

CHAPTER 7
Post Production

● ● ●

It is interesting to briefly, and by no means exhaustively, take a look at what happened to some of the cast and crew who worked with Wayne on his lost films. Typically, some aspired to greater things, and certainly both Robert Stack and James Arness went on to establish long and successful careers. Others seemed to fall by the wayside after only the briefest flirtations with Hollywood.

ACTORS AND ACTRESSES

Walter Abel's (Col. Fuller in *Island in the Sky*) last film credit was *Mirage* (1965), directed by Edward Dmytryk and starring Gregory Peck. He received extensive critical and public attention for his role as a doomed industrialist in the picture. He kept busy on stage and television productions throughout the 1950s. Abel was appointed president of the American National Theatre and Academy. His last screen performance was opposite Katharine Hepburn in *The Ultimate Solution of Grace Quigley* (1984). He died of a heart attack on March 26, 1987.

James Arness is the brother of actor Peter Graves. Arness auditioned for the part of Matt Dillon in *Gunsmoke* after taking advice from his friend John Wayne, who eventually released him from his contract with Batjac when he was offered the part.
    Between 1959 and 1961, Arness was associate producer of the show. Today Arness keeps busy with many off-screen activities.

Doe Avedon—despite John Wayne's high hopes for this talented newcomer, very little else was heard of her. In 1954 she costarred in the musical *Deep in My Heart* with Jose Ferrer and Merle Oberon, and in 1956 appeared in *The Boss* opposite John Payne. Early in 1957 she played Mike McCall in the original pilot for *The Penthouse* with Lori Nelson (in the role of Greta Hanson) and Charlotte Austin (Loco Jones). The original pilot was not successful and never aired. Lori Nelson was the only one of the girls recalled when another pilot of the show was made.

Dawn Bender's last, and only other, credit was in *The Actress* (1953).

William Campbell played young Hobie Wheeler in *The High and the Mighty* but also starred in many episodes of the original *Star Trek* television series. Campbell remains a friend of the Wayne family and says, "John Wayne cared about his family, and his legacy takes care of his descendants." Presumably this is why these two films, the last in the Wayne vault to be released, were held and protected for so many years.

For the fans, however, they were held for far too long. Campbell goes on,

> I spoke to Michael about them a number of times. You may know, he managed to put a very clean print together. It was damaged in a flood. He told me that one of the ways he completed the cutting of this present copy is that some of the guys who worked in the lab there had run a copy of their own off the master.
>
> Michael had to go back to find these guys to retrieve the portions which had been lost. And he did so. He keeps telling me that he's got plans for it, and I tell him, "The fact of the matter is, there's not a pilot in the country who wouldn't buy a tape of it. It will go like hot cakes." It was the best of the commercial airline disaster pictures. There's no doubt about it. And then there's the music. I think the family must own it all, they, and whoever the other partners were. So they must own the music. That score is one of the great standards.
>
> I told Mike, "You've got a number of people still alive from the picture. You could release it as a special run." They could have a mini-premiere. I've thought many times about having a *High and Mighty* convention. I think it would draw a hell of a lot of people.

Harry Carey Jr., a good friend of Wayne's, continues to work on a variety of projects. His filmography includes roles in *Last Stand at Saber River* (1997), *Ben Johnson: Third Cowboy on the Right* (1996), *The Sunchaser* (1996), *Wyatt Earp: Return to Tombstone* (1994), *Tombstone* (1993), *The Exorcist III* (1990) and *Back to the Future Part III* (1990).

Laraine Day was born on October 13, 1917. Her acting career began after her parents moved to Long Beach, California, where she joined the Long Beach Players. She appeared in her first film in 1937 in a bit part and then starred in several George O'Brien Westerns. After signing a contract with MGM, she achieved popularity playing the part of Nurse Lamont in that studio's Dr. Kildare series. An attractive, engaging performer, she had leads in several medium-budget films for various studios but never achieved major stardom. She was married for thirteen years to baseball manager Leo Durocher and took such an active interest in his career and the sport of baseball that she became known as "The First Lady of Baseball."

Andy Devine was born on October 7, 1905, and died of leukemia on February 18, 1977. He continued to work right up until his death. He starred as Marshal Appleyard opposite Wayne in *The Man Who Shot Liberty Valence* in 1963 but was probably best known as the voice of Friar Tuck in the Disney animated film *Robin Hood* (1973). Andy's voice was so well-known it was insured by Lloyds of London for half a million dollars.

Ann Doran, who played fragile Mrs. Joseph in *The High and the Mighty*, and who also had a small part in *Island in the Sky*, followed her two Wayne-Fellows productions with plenty of television work. Her last appearance was in *The A-Team* in 1986.

The prolific veteran actress, born in 1911, established an extensive résumé spanning five decades and has credits in more than 200 films and 1,000 TV shows. She is perhaps best remembered for her role as James Dean's mother in 1955's *Rebel Without a Cause*. She died on September 19, 2000, after suffering a series of strokes.

Paul Fix, a close friend of John Wayne, was one of the busiest and most versatile character actors in Hollywood, making more than three hundred films during his career—twenty six of those with Wayne. The role he will probably be best remembered for is that of Micah Torrance, the easy-going sheriff of North Fork, in the television series *The Rifleman* (1958). He played invalid Frank Briscoe in *The High and the Mighty*. He was born March 13, 1901, and died October 14, 1983, of kidney failure.

Allyn Joslyn died of heart failure on January 21, 1981. He had a successful television career, starring in *Where's Raymond*. He made his last film, a Western starring John Astin, *The Brothers O'Toole*, in 1973.

Sean McClory, the Irish character actor best known for his role in John Wayne's *The Quiet Man*, died December 10, 2003, at seventy-nine. McClory began acting in Galway, Ireland, and was a member of the prestigious Abbey Theatre in Dublin.

RKO studios brought him to the United States in 1947 as a contract player. He slowly worked his way up to larger parts in such films as *The Quiet Man, Island in the Sky* (1953), and *Charade* (1953). In the late '50s, he appeared in the television series

The Californians in the role of storekeeper Jack McGivern. In the 1960s he made several television appearances while his movie work waned. Among the series he appeared on were *The Virginian, Daniel Boone, The High Chaparral, Mannix, The Outer Limits,* and *Bonanza.* His final film role was in the 1987 John Huston drama *The Dead.*

Lloyd Nolan died September 27, 1985. He played Pilot Stutz in *Island in the Sky.*

He had a long list of film and television credits but always confounded those who predicted major stardom. His talent seems to have been largely taken for granted.

Robert Stack died on May 14, 2003, following a heart attack. He was eighty-four.

After being warned by Wayne that Wellman would get him sooner or later, the emotional Stack recalled hiding from the director on a number of occasions during the filming of *The High and the Mighty.*

Stack made over forty-five films and starred as Eliot Ness in a hundred episodes of *The Untouchables.* He also narrated more than 1,200 *Unsolved Mysteries.*

Carl Switzer was born on August 7, 1927. He became a child star, known as Alfalfa through the *Our Gang* movies. Switzer had minor roles in both of the lost movies. He was shot dead on January 21, 1959, by a friend in a dispute over money. Switzer was demanding repayment of fifty dollars that he thought his friend, Stiltz, owed him. Stiltz denied murder and said he shot Switzer in self-defense.

Jan Sterling, born April 3, 1921, in New York, had intended to establish a long and glittering career when she signed up to work alongside John Wayne and admitted, "I adored Hollywood because I'd always wanted to be a movie star. Maybe in some funny, Freudian way, it was my way of getting more attention than my baby sister, who was pretty with curly hair. We all have drives we don't completely understand." But while the talented, stick-thin, and sullen 1950s actress did go on to win many roles in films and television series, Sterling never did quite reach the top echelon of stardom.

She involved herself in a variety of humanitarian causes and through the 1970s entered into a strong personal relationship actor Sam Wanamaker. They never married but stayed together until his death in 1993. Inactive for nearly two decades, Sterling, then age eighty, made an appearance at the Cinecon Film Festival in Los Angeles in the fall of 2001. On March 26, 2004, Jan Sterling passed away after a series of strokes at the Motion Picture and Television Hospital in Woodland Hills, California. She was eighty-three.

Born in 1910, **Claire Trevor** died at ninety of respiratory ailments at her home in Newport Beach, California, on April 8, 2000. She appeared in more than sixty motion pictures opposite many of Hollywood's leading men, including John Wayne, Humphrey Bogart, Spencer Tracy, Clark Gable, Edward G. Robinson, and William Holden, and said, "Don't fall in love with your leading man. Of course, that's just what I did."

A three-time Oscar nominee, Trevor won the Best Supporting Actress award for her 1948 performance in *Key Largo*, costarring with Humphrey Bogart, Edward G. Robinson, and Lauren Bacall. In 1956, Trevor won an Emmy for Best Live Television Performance by an Actress for *Dodsworth*, with Fredric March, on NBC's *Producer's Showcase*.

Her career spanned several decades of success in radio, stage, and television. She was renowned for playing molls, floozies, and broads and was cast as the owner of a rowdy saloon in many a Western. Again in *The High and the Mighty*, she starred as a hard-boiled blond with a heart of gold.

A passionate advocate for the arts and arts education, she established The Claire Trevor School of Arts at the University of California, Irvine, after retiring from acting.

Phyllis Winger has no other credit except as a handmaiden in the 1950 picture *Princess of the Nile*.

TECHNICIANS

During his life, **William Wellman** was better known for his larger-than-life personality than his prolific career as a film director. A Wellman film set was more often than not witness to fistfights, wild parties, and daring stunts (all of which usually involved the director himself). Many actors disliked his method of bullying a performance out of them, and he had even argued with Wayne during the making of *The High and the Mighty*.

The Hollywood establishment didn't like him, and Irene Selznick (first wife to David Selznick and daughter to Louis B. Mayer) referred to him as "a terror, a shoot-up-the-town fellow, trying to be a great big, masculine I-don't-know-what. David had a real weakness for him. I didn't share it."

Wellman said, "I couldn't stand being an actor. I haven't liked many actors anyway, and I've directed most of them. One of my sons is an actor, and it breaks my heart, but there's nothing I can do about it." Of course, it was the director himself who introduced his son to the world of acting through *The High and the Mighty*.

Wellman was born in Brookline, Massachusetts, on the leap year date February 29, 1896. Like many of his contemporaries (and unlike today's filmmakers), he got his education not from college or film school but from living life to the full. In his stories, character relationships, and filmmaking technique, *common sense* is the watchword. Wellman's characters may occasionally do crazy, irresponsible things, but they always do them for very good reasons, a reason Wayne himself loved Wild Bill.

Wellman commented about his craft, "The best director is the director whose handprints are not on the film."

He died on December 9, 1975, from leukemia.

Andrew McLaglen concentrated his talent directing outdoor films, specializing in Westerns and adventures especially for Wayne's production company. His work in the film industry was consistently entertaining and commercial.

Following *The High and the Mighty*, he went on to make his solo directorial debut with *Gun the Man Down* (1956). He worked steadily throughout the late 1950s, the 1960s, and the 1970s before turning to television, where he became a prolific director on shows such as *Perry Mason*, *Rawhide*, and *Have Gun—Will Travel*, among others. He was the principal director of *Gunsmoke* during its early years on the air.

Epilogue

● ● ●

Jon **Wayne** enjoyed more than fifty years of creating screen heroes, many of whom are indelibly etched into the consciousness of the Western world. Sadly, two of his most heroic portrayals are among the least well-known of his illustrious career. As Dooley, the captain of the downed Corsair, and as Dan Roman, he generated a couple of characters that could easily have stood alongside Nathan Brittles, John Stryker, Ringo Kid, Sean Thornton, and J. B. Books. Until now they have remained no more than footnotes in the Wayne tapestry of screen legends because, until recently, few people had seen either film or character since their original 1950s release dates.

As products of Duke's Wayne-Fellows production company (which evolved into Batjac), the films were two of three releases of the era (the other being *Hondo*), to which the Wayne estate retained full ownership rights. Although *Hondo* was finally released some years ago for public consumption, and the restoration and distribution of *The High and the Mighty* was long discussed, both pictures remained parts of an intriguing Hollywood mystery. They have been hidden away in the Wayne vaults, supreme examples of Michael Wayne's theory that "less is more." Michael Wayne believed that the longer the two highly sought titles were withheld from the public, the greater would become their desire and the more valuable the films would become. In 1995 the head of Wayne Enterprises, established to control John Wayne's image, confirmed that he didn't want to put either film into syndication: "If the public wants to see a picture it hasn't seen for a long time, there is more impact with a periodic release."

This philosophy may have some merit when you talk about a year or two. But as decade followed decade deep into the millennium, the policy might have proved a dangerous one, promising diminishing returns. As each day went by there were fewer and fewer of us who actually remembered seeing the films first time around. John Wayne fans were certainly not getting any younger.

Add to this the fact that, of the three movies Michael chose to hold back, *Island in the Sky* was a modest production, shot in black and white and without all the fanfare of 3-D or CinemaScope, and was necessarily thrown into the category of one of Wayne's lesser film projects. That was a shame because, low budget and all, the film, especially Wayne's mighty portrayal of Dooley, is worthy of more respect. And even though the music from *The High and the Mighty* became instantly recognizable as Wayne's theme tune for all his later public appearances, including his last performance at the 1979 Oscar ceremony, that theme, along with both movies, was sadly shelved for far too long.

As recently as 2003, Andrew McLaglen admitted that certainly Wayne himself intended his films to be seen and enjoyed—not withheld. Maureen O'Hara also seems to back that view: "Duke was so sentimental about his pictures, like old friendships." It seems unlikely that he would have appreciated seeing these two gems buried away as they were.

And the mystery raged over them for so long. There were definitely some difficult technical problems concerned with restoration and conversion, but more importantly there was a proliferation of legal wrangling between Warner Bros. and Wayne Enterprises over actual ownership and distribution rights. Part of the problem over the copyrights for *Island in the Sky* and *The High and the Mighty* may even date back to the winding up of Wayne-Fellows and the formation of Wayne's independent company, Batjac. When his partnership ended with Robert Fellows in 1954, the rights to several films that Wayne-Fellows had made were all worked out, but unfortunately *Island in the Sky* and *The High and the Mighty* were both excluded from those contracts. It has never been clear why that happened, but the confusion left Warner Bros. in a position such that it was able to scrap over rerelease distribution.

In the 1970s Warners wanted to release both films to television, but Batjac prevented them from doing so. From that point on the relationship between Wayne Enterprises and Warner Bros. deteriorated, and the legal wrangling spread to VHS and DVD rights.

For a short time in the 1980s both films could be rented in an old 16mm format at certain film clubs and at college film schools. But when bootleg copies began emerging, both films were pulled from Warners' catalog, and apart from very poor quality pirate copies (presumably made from the 16mm tapes), they were never again seen until the U.S. release of both films in 2005.

Before that date rumor and counter-rumor abounded, but nothing definitive ever seemed to materialize. Promises of release were made and broken, and expectations were raised and dashed in a very messy and protracted way. Internet message boards and clubs were awash with demands to see "the Wayne estate's hostages," and the comments were a clear demonstration of the fans' desire to get hold of both these films. People from all over the world clamored for information.

Film critic Leonard Maltin, who called *The High and the Mighty* "The Holy Grail of all John Wayne movies," said that following the untimely death of Michael Wayne there was an increased demand for the two films to be taken out of mothballs. "Ask anyone who writes about videos, and they will tell you that the film they most often get asked about is *The High and the Mighty*."

Over the years Wayne Enterprises received several substantial offers to take them out of the vault, and since all the income raised by Wayne Enterprises goes directly to the John Wayne Cancer Institute, the release of the two films was destined to generate a nice healthy profit to go in that direction. Maltin explained, "The films are worth real money; this is not a little crumb or some niche market for old movies. They have worldwide appeal."

In January 2004 there was obvious movement behind the scenes, and Amazon.com noted briefly, "Wayne pix to be restored. *High and Mighty* and *Island* to get homevid release." Michael Fleming wrote, "The estate of John Wayne has made a deal with Cinetech and Chace Productions to update and restore the two 1950s hits. Arrangement was made with Gretchen Wayne, the widow of the actor's late son, Michael. Move came as a result of a volume of calls by fans who wanted to see the films."

At the same time that notice was posted on Amazon, other sites noted that it was Warners who finally acquired the rights and that it was they who would release the films to coincide exactly with the fiftieth anniversary of the making of *The High and the Mighty*.

In the end, the privilege of releasing "new" John Wayne titles fell to Paramount. And in the end, Wayne's son Michael may just about have been right: "Less is more." The demand was strengthened, and now the public is reveling in seeing the two lost films again. The Special Edition DVDs are selling like hotcakes, and they have created Amazon bestsellers. Those too young to understand the Wayne phenomenon seem to have been shocked at how well they have been selling on DVD but forget that these discs present the movies on home video for the first time ever. The twenty-five-year wait obviously served its purpose among film fans—particularly those with a love for John Wayne—and as one Amazon reviewer noted, "This is Our Guy topping the charts nearly thirty years after his death."

Other DVD reviews posted on Amazon include:

> Check your memory at the door—not your brain—it's a smart flick. Clichés become cliches for a reason. They become clichés because they're repeated, and they're repeated because initially they worked so well they bear repeating. *The High and the Mighty* is not clichéd. It created the cliché because it's just that good. Every disaster movie since has stolen its formula of assembling potential victims dealing with conflicts later resolved when examined within the context of facing one's mortality. So watch the film within the context of its time: Ike's in the white house, Elvis is still an unknown truck driver, and Democrats don't hate America.
>
> Be prepared: Dmitri Tomkin's [*sic*] Oscar-winning score will stick in your head as insidiously as the "The Girl From Ipanema."
>
> Claire Trevor's in the film. Yup, The Ringo Kid and Dallas together again. Unfortunately, they only share a few lines of exposition together, but it's still there. Fifteen years after *Stagecoach* and it's still there. Duke flashes that crooked Ringo smile he'd

never lose, and Claire still creates her fallen angel using nothing but her eyes. It's a lovely moment for Wayne fans. There are others, but I'm not gonna pull a Maltin.

Now you have to watch *Airplane* again. The funniest film since Groucho died is actually funnier after seeing *The High and the Mighty*. Robert Stack's in both. Need I say more?

*   *   *

Garfield pressed the collar of his coat tighter around his throat . . . he lingered uncertainly, looking after Dan Roman, who was already a hazy figure through the rain. Seen from a distance, his slight limp appeared more pronounced as he carefully avoided the glistening puddles on the concrete.

"So long . . . you ancient pelican. . . ."

Then as he turned for a last look at the sky, he heard the distant sound of a man whistling. He found it very satisfying.

—from the novel *The High and the Mighty*

Bibliography

BOOKS AND VIDEOS

Davis, Ronald L. *Duke: The Life and Image of John Wayne*. Norman, OK: University of Oklahoma Press, 1988.

Gann, Ernest K. *Island in the Sky*. New York: Viking Press, 1944.

_____. *A Hostage to Fortune*. New York: Knopf, 1978.

_____. *The High and the Mighty*. New York: Sloane, 1953.

Levy, Emanuel. *John Wayne: Prophet of the American Way of Life*. Metuchen, NJ: Scarecrow Press, 1988.

Ricci, Mark, Steve Zmijewsky, and Boris Zmijewsky. *The Complete Films of John Wayne*. Secaucus, NJ: Citadel Press, 1983.

Roberts, Randy, and James S. Olson. *John Wayne: American*. Lincoln, NB: University of Nebraska Press, 1995.

Robinson, Todd. *Wild Bill: Hollywood Maverick; The Life and Times of William A. Wellman*. VHS. Directed by Todd Robinson. New York: Kino International, 1996.

Schickel, Richard. *The Men Who Made the Movies: Interviews with Frank Capra, George Cukor, Howard Hawks, Alfred Hitchcock, Vincente Minnelli, King Vidor, Raoul Walsh, and William A. Wellman*. New York: Atheneum, 1975.

Stack, Robert. *Straight Shooting*. With Mark Evans. New York: Macmillan, 1980.

Wills, Garry. *John Wayne's America: The Politics of Celebrity*. New York: Simon and Schuster, 1997.

Zolotow, Maurice. *Shooting Star: A Biography of John Wayne*. New York: Simon and Schuster, 1974.

ARTICLES, CLIPPINGS, ORAL HISTORIES, AND OTHER REFERENCE MATERIAL

The Warner Brothers Papers held by the University of Southern California, School of Cinema-Television, including production notes and clippings, press books, article on career of Archie Stout, Doe Avedon, and Jan Sterling, dialogue transcripts, letters of Robert Fellows and John Wayne, Joseph Breen (VP and director Production Code Administration).

James Arness File, Margaret Herrick Library, Academy of Motion Picture Arts and
    Sciences, Beverly Hills, California.
Harry Carey Jr. File, Margaret Herrick Library.
Harry Carey Jr. Oral History held at Southern Methodist University, Dallas, Texas.
Laraine Day Oral History Interview by Barbara Hall, Margaret Herrick Library.
Laraine Day Oral History held at Southern Methodist University.
Andy Devine File, Margaret Herrick Library.
Robert Fellows File, Margaret Herrick Library.
Paul Fix File, Margaret Herrick Library.
Andrew McLaglen File, Margaret Herrick Library.
Andrew McLaglen Oral History held at Southern Methodist University.
Lloyd Nolan Oral History, Southern Methodist University.
Robert Stack Oral History, Southern Methodist University.
Claire Trevor File, Margaret Herrick Library.
John Wayne File, Margaret Herrick Library.
William Wellman File, Margaret Herrick Library.

*   *   *

Academy of Motion Picture Arts and Sciences, selection of reviews and cuttings on
    Island in the Sky and *The High and the Mighty*.
American Cinematographer, article on William Clothier, August 1986.
American Classic Screen, article on William Wellman, Summer 1980.
American Classic Screen, article on William Wellman, Winter 1980.
British Film Institute, notes on William H. Clothier.
Campfire Embers, interview by Tim Lilley with William Campbell.
Film Dope, article on Andrew McLaglen, June 1987.
Film West, article on the legacy of Wellman, October 1998.
Filmmaker's Newsletter, interview with William Clothier, April 1973.
Films in Review, article on Wellman, May 1982.
Films in Review, memories of Wellman, January/February 1997.
Hollywood Reporter, August 7, 1953.
Hollywood Reporter (UK), December 24, 1953.
Hollywood Reporter, May 27, 1954.
Kinematograph (UK), September 1954.
Los Angeles County Museum of Art, essay from Magill's Survey of Cinema, 1983.
Monthly Film Bulletin   (UK), October 1954.
Motion Picture Herald (UK), May 1954.
Motion Picture Herald, article on Andrew McLaglen, February 1967.
MovieMaker, "How I Got to Call the Shots: An Interview with Burt Kennedy," 2002.

National Film Theatre, audiotape interview with William Wellman.
Photoplay, article on James Arness, October 1973.
Photoplay, interview with Andy Devine, May 1974.
Today's Cinema (UK), September 1953.
Today's Cinema (UK), September 1954.
United Artists, biography of Andrew V. McLaglen.
Variety, article on Andrew McLaglen, June 20, 1979.

Index